CONTINENTAL PILSENER

DAVID MILLER

(Bp) A Brewers Publications Book

Continental Pilsener
By Dave Miller
Classic Beer Style Series
Edited by Virginia Thomas
Copyright 1990 by Dave Miller

ISBN 0-937381-20-9
Printed in the United States of America
10 9 8 7 6 5 4

Published by Brewers Publications,
a division of the Association of Brewers, Inc.
PO Box 1679, Boulder, Colorado 80306-1679USA
(303) 447-0816 • FAX: (303) 447-2825

Direct all inquiries/orders to the above address.

Cover design by Robert L. Schram
Cover photography by Michael Lichter, Michael Lichter Photography

Table of Contents

Acknowledgements and Dedication

I want first of all to thank Storey Communications, Inc., for granting permission to include in this book recipes from my *Complete Handbook of Home Brewing*.

I also want to thank Charlie Papazian for conceiving of the *Classic Beer Style Series* and asking me to participate in it. Over the last decade and a half, he has done more than anyone in this country to promote the appreciation of fine beer and encourage small-scale brewing.

I owe a special debt to all the authors listed in the bibliography, and the hundreds of brewmasters who stand behind them. Their work has made it possible for us to brew better beers today than ever before.

I also want to thank my wife and children for their patience with me during the writing of this book and their unfailing support of my brewing ambitions.

Finally, special thanks to George Fix for his many hours of generous assistance and good fellowship. I am proud to acknowledge my debt to his vast understanding of brewing science. Still, as fine a brewer as he is, he is a finer human being. This book is dedicated to him, with gratitude and admiration.

Brewers Publications would like to thank the following companies and individuals for letting us use their photographs:

Michael Lichter, page 2
Phil Markowski, pages 6, 13
George Rivers, pages 9, 69, 72
Charlie Papazian, page 19
Ian Priddey, pages 35, 61
Campaign for Real Ale (CAMRA), pages 47, 60

About the Author

Dave Miller is a native of St. Louis, Mo., where he still lives with his wife and children. He brewed his first batch of beer in 1975. In 1981 he won the title Hombrewer of the Year when his Dutch Pilsner was judged Best of Show at the American Homebrewers Assocation national competition. That same year, his first book, *Home Brewing for Americans*, was published. This was the first American book to deal with advanced all-grain brewing techniques.

Dave is a charter member of the St. Louis Brews homebrewing club and served for two years as its vice president, designing brewing projects, making presentations, and writing a monthly column for the club newsletter. He credits his club members with inspiring him to write *The Complete Handbook of Home Brewing*, which was published in November 1988. He has also written several articles for *zymurgy* magazine.

A former teacher, Dave has most recently been involved in lobbying the Missouri legislature for passage of a bill legalizing brewpubs. With the recent enactment of that measure, his current project is to found the first St. Louis brewpub and become its brewmaster.

Introduction

Pilsener is the dominant beer style in the world today. From Milwaukee to Brussels and Juarez to Manila, beers brewed in every part of the planet proudly bear the label "Pils" or "Pilsener," a tribute to the city of Plzeň, Czechoslovakia, where this style originated more than one hundred and fifty years ago. Many brand names also reflect the style's nation of origin: National Bohemian beer once was brewed in Pennsylvania, and today you can find on the shelves of American supermarkets Bohemia beer brewed in Mexico. To be sure, not all of these beers live up to their heritage. Many of those brewed in North America and the Orient are pallid imitations with only a superficial resemblance to the genuine Pils. Still, the very fact that so many brewers make a Pilsener-style product is testimony to the reputation of the Bohemian brewers and the impact their creation has had on the world of brewing.

Probably the best evidence of Pilsener's appeal has been its influence on the brewing industry of Munich, where lager brewing originated. Munich's proud tradition has been rooted in a very different style of beer—dark, sweet, aromatic Münchner. In the 1920s, when applied chemistry had

Prague's first and most famous tavern, U Flecků, dates back to 1499 and brews its own beer.

advanced to the point where brewers could make both light- and dark-colored beers from the same water, the Munich brewers introduced a new style of Munich beer. The new beer was similar to the original but pale in color and obviously designed to compete with the Pilsener lagers that had gained so much popularity. Today this pale Münchner, often called *Helles*, is the everyday drink of Bavarians. The Munich breweries also have started making their own Pilseners, and world beer authority Michael Jackson was bemused to find the great Spaten brewery touting its Pilsener as "our best beer!"

I first became acquainted with genuine, European Pilsener in Hamburg, Germany, in 1971. I went into a restaurant and a waiter, assuming that I was American and would want a light-colored beer, asked if I wanted Pilsener. "Ja," I answered, not really sure what he meant or even why he was asking the question. Weren't all beers Pilseners?

I don't believe I had ever tasted a European lager before, and that one was a revelation. Presented in the classic, tall, conical Pilsener glass, the beer had a depth of flavor I had never encountered. The stinging, flowery hop aroma was an enticing prelude to the rich, malty sweetness of the flavor, which was perfectly balanced by its bitterness. I drained the first one and ordered a second. Eighteen years later, I still credit that German Pilsener as the beginning of my serious involvement with the brewer's art.

I still feel a special affection for a good Pilsener, and with the passage of time I appreciate its virtues even more. It is light without being insipid or bland; hoppy, yet smooth and mellow. It is simultaneously refreshing and immensely satisfying—two characteristics that may seem to be mutually exclusive and that are not, in my opinion, so successfully combined in any other beer style. At the same time, Pilsener is not a "big" or "complex" brew that brims with esters and other fermentation byproducts. It has a clean, simple flavor profile that makes it an ideal accompaniment for many types of food. It is a drink for all occasions, and I believe it is this adaptability that has made it the most popular beer today in the nations of Northern and Central Europe.

1

History

Since its beginnings in the mid-nineteenth century, the popularity and evolution of Pilsener have paralleled the technological developments of recent history. The worldwide popularity of lager beer in general, and Pilsener in particular, would not have been possible without the development of transportation, refrigeration, and other basic industries. And while beer cannot be held accountable for the follies and triumphs of the modern world, it has contributed some of its minor advances.

In Europe, the eighteenth century marked the beginning of the industrial revolution, when scientific discoveries were applied to the problems of humans. Starting in England, brewing was transformed from a cottage industry into a large-scale manufacturing operation with a consequent need for product consistency. Progressive brewers brought the thermometer and hydrometer (or saccharometer) into service in the brewery. While "old-timers" first resisted the devices as a disparagement of their skill, these new tools eventually were accepted because they were more reliable than the old methods. The end result was better beer.

At this time, Czech-speaking lands were basically

The main entrance of the Pilsner Urquell Brewery (right) and the adjacent hotel and restaurant (left), Plzeň, Czechoslovakia.

agrarian, with beer and its raw ingredients an integral part of the national society and economy. Bohemian and Moravian summer or two-row barleys (especially the Hanna and Kniefl varieties) were then, as they are now, among the most prized in the world, and the famous western Bohemian hop, the Zatec Red or Saaz, is arguably the finest grown anywhere. Aware that its hops were a national treasure, for centuries the Grand Dukes of Bohemia attempted to prevent the export of their precious herbs and actually mandated the death penalty for anyone caught smuggling the rhizomes (root cuttings) out of the country. Then, during the last part of the eighteenth century and the beginning of the nineteenth, František Ondřej Poupe, a Bohemian brewmaster, brought modern standards and techniques to Bohemia's brewing industry and thus prepared it for its coming prominence.

By 1840, Bohemia possessed the know-how and raw materials for making first-class beers. But fermentation still utilized mixed cultures of top-fermenting yeast, and in many places, including Plzeň, the results were inconsistent at best. At about this time, the citizens of the town resolved to build a new brewery in the hope that it would make better beer than the old one did. But exactly at this time, the long-held secret of Munich—bottom fermentation—was revealed. While the function of yeast was still not understood, the new generation of Bavarian brewers had begun to realize that yeast was the key to the success of their methods and the quality of their beer. In 1842, a Bavarian monk smuggled a pot of bottom-fermenting yeast into Bohemia and supplied the last missing element for the creation of a new beer. This was the beginning of the "lager revolution" and the beginning of the style we now call Pilsener.

SUCCESS AND CHANGE

Since then, the story of Pilsener has been one of unparalleled success and the changes success can bring. The method for brewing light, well-carbonated lagers spread quickly across Northern Europe, through Germany, and into the Low Countries and Scandinavia. Germans and other Central Europeans immigrating to the New World brought with them their brewing skills. As early as 1850, these new arrivals began brewing lager in Canada and the United States. Later waves of immigrants reinforced the trend, and in North America the terms "lager" and "Pilsener" became almost synonymous.

This growth in popularity brought changes as brewers adapted the style to fit their local conditions and shifting popular taste. In creating Pilsener, the brewery in Plzeň had exploited not only the region's excellent malt and hops, but also its water supply, which is almost unique among the great brewing centers of Europe. The water there is extremely soft—total dissolved solids are under 50 parts per million (ppm)—and this characteristic makes it possible to brew a pale beer with a very high hop rate, a combination that is almost impossible with hard water. In other cities, brewers who attempted to duplicate the Plzeň beer found that they had to lower their hop rates and make other changes in order to get the mellow flavor they wanted. The clean, refreshing palate of good Pilsener became so desirable that rich flavors were muted in order to emphasize this characteristic. Carbonation sometimes was increased slightly, and adjuncts such as corn and rice were introduced later in order to lighten the body.

To regress a little bit, these changes did not take place abruptly but rather evolved. In Germany, the Reinheitsgebot (purity law) forbade the use of adjuncts; yet even there, Pilsener beers were brewed to be lighter and less malty than the original Pilsener. The German Pilseners often had a lower hop rate, partly owing, as previously noted, to the water. Different brewing methods were also employed. In Plzeň, the brewery used a traditional triple-decoction mash similar to that employed at Munich. This process was as time-consuming and intensive then as it is today and tended to increase the color of the finished beer. As a result, German brewers usually adopted a shorter, double-decoction system that produced a paler beer. Another change that also lightened the beer was the use of pressurized steam to heat the brewing kettles, since direct firing almost always scorches the wort and caramelizes it to some extent. This innovation—pioneered in Munich in the latter half of the nineteenth century—not only improved working conditions in the brewhouse, but also improved the consistency and flavor of the beer.

The Wernesgrüner brewery in Thuringia, East Germany, traces its roots back to 1436.

SCIENTIFIC AND ENGINEERING ADVANCES

The "lager revolution" began before Louis Pasteur had demonstrated the true nature of fermentation, but it certainly would not have succeeded without him. Pilsener owes its world-wide popularity to the development of brewing science and adequate microbiological controls. More than almost any other style of beer, a light lager such as Pilsener leaves no margin for the ruinous effects of infection. Pasteur's classic investigations of beer and wine fermentations not only revealed for the first time the true role of yeast, but also demonstrated that off-flavors are often the result of other organisms.

Pasteur's discoveries led directly to the work of another great microbiologist, Emil Hansen, who worked at the Carlsberg brewery in Copenhagen. In 1881, Hansen developed techniques for isolating and propagating single yeast cells. This ability to produce pure cultures of selected yeast strains put brewers in control of their product for the first time. Up to that point, as Hansen discovered, all yeasts were a mixture of strains, some good for brewing, some not so good, and all were more or less contaminated with bacteria and wild yeast. It was mostly a matter of luck if the good yeast managed to dominate a fermentation and thereby produce an acceptable beer. But using Hansen's methods, brewers could select a yeast strain according to their requirements, just as they did their malts and hops. It is hard to overestimate the importance of this development in the success of lager brewing in general and the Pilsener style in particular.

As I previously mentioned, developments in engineering also played a part in the evolution of Pilsener. The great German brewmaster Gabriel Sedelmayr, chief brewer at the Spaten brewery in Munich during the mid-1800s, was perhaps the greatest advocate of steam in the brewery, but he deserves even more credit for his role in the development of refrigeration. Indeed, he could be called the father of the brewing revolution, since refrigeration turned lager brewing into an operation that could be carried on year-round, independent of climate or terrain. Prior to the introduction of artificial cooling, brewing could be done only during winter, and lagering had to be done in natural caves, which limited the sites on which a brewery could be built.

As Pilsener brewing spread across Europe, adjuncts were introduced into the process in Scandinavia and the Low Countries. This alteration brought with it a totally new mashing system: the so-called "mixed mash," described on page 15. But of far greater significance is the lightening of body and flavor that this technique made possible. The refreshing quality of the beer was thereby emphasized. To keep everything in balance, the hop rate usually was adjusted downward somewhat, but this depended on the water and, of course, the judgment of the brewer. So strong has been the drive towards adjuncts that, in more recent times, some North German brewers have evaded the spirit (though not the letter) of the Reinheitsgebot by using a proportion of "chit malt" in the grist. This is barley malt so undermodified that for all practical purposes it is identical to the raw grain.

American-style Pilseners employed many of the same innovations as those used in Scandinavia. The difference is one of degree. Faced with rather coarse-flavored native hops and high-tannin, six-row barley, the New World brewers carried the tendency to lighten both the malt and hop character of the beer to the greatest extreme. Over the decades, American beer has become more and more delicate in its bouquet and body.

THE RESULTS OF SUCCESS

As a result of its evolution, Pilsener has become a style with such a range of flavor profiles—from rich, malty and hoppy to almost bland—that it can only be characterized by four common characteristics: pale color, relatively high carbonation, a flavor well-balanced between malt and hops with neither predominating and, finally, bottom fermentation that allows a "clean" aroma in which the basic ingredients (rather than yeast by-products) prevail. But this last characteristic is arguable since it is really common to almost all types of lager beer.

SUBSTYLES OF BEER

No description of Pilsener would be complete without listing the substyles into which it has evolved. Having outlined the history behind their development, I will now briefly describe how they are made today, and how the differences in formulation and production methods affect the flavor of the finished product.

- Pilsner Urquell -

Pilsner Urquell (in Czech, *Plzeňsky Prazdroj*) is the original Pilsener beer, and it has changed little since 1870 or 1880, when the technology of the brewery was fixed. The beer is brewed in small batches of around 152 U.S. barrels (180 hectoliters) from a blend of two-row malts, using the triple-decoction mash system. The malt is considerably undermodified by American or German standards, which makes a lengthy mash necessary. The crushed malt is mashed-in with cold water, then infused with boiling water to raise the temperature to 95 degrees F (35 degrees C). Subsequent rests are made at temperatures of 122, 149, and 165 degrees F (50, 65, and 74 degrees C). After lautering, the wort is boiled in direct-fired copper kettles for two hours and

Postcard from the original Pilsener brewery, Plzeňsky Prazdroj, or Pilsner Urquell.

hopping takes place in three stages. The wort is cooled in two stages, first passing through a closed counterflow chiller and then a large flat copper pan (coolship) where the trub settles and the wort absorbs oxygen. The yeast is pitched at about 40 degrees F (4 degrees C), and fermentation lasts twelve to fourteen days at a temperature near 46 degrees F (8 degrees C). The beer is then transferred to the lagering vats and kraeusened. It is stored for a full three months at temperatures near the freezing point. The beer is filtered before being kegged or bottled. The bottled beer is pasteurized, with beer destined for North America receiving a longer treatment to increase its stability.

Pilsner Urquell is noted for its light golden color and rich maltiness. The best way to describe it is perhaps to say that it has a little more of everything—sweetness, bitterness, and hop nose—than the average Pilsener beer. Flavor will be described in greater detail in the next chapter.

- All-Malt Continental Pilseners -

Other Czech Pilseners are hard to find in the United States, but German versions are relatively commonplace. The Dortmunder Actien Brauerei (DAB) brews an excellent example of Pilsener that is marketed in this country under the label DAB. All-malt Pilseners also are brewed in Poland, Belgium, Holland, and other European countries. Premium two-row barleys are used almost exclusively, but the trend is to make a well-modified malt rather than the undermodified type used at Plzeň. This goes along with the shorter mash schedules mentioned earlier. A double-decoction mash, with mashing-in at around 122 degrees F (50 degrees C), is common in Germany, though the trend is toward even shorter methods such as the single-decoction or upward-infusion (temperature programmed) systems.

14

Boiling times may be as little as an hour. The finished beer is usually yellow rather than golden, with a lighter malt flavor as a result of both the malts and the process employed. Because they often are brewed from harder water, these Pilseners have a bitterness that is lower than that of Pilsner Urquell, but higher than American-style Pilsener. They usually retain the strong hop character of the original, including the unique aroma of Saaz hops. (More than half of Czechoslovakia's annual production of hops is exported.) Two or three hop additions are usual, with some brewers adding hops to the hop back or fermenter (a process called "dry hopping") to get the freshest possible aroma. Fermentation is usually briefer, with the temperature being allowed to rise during the process from around 48 degrees F (9 degrees C) at pitching to perhaps as high as 60 degrees F (15 degrees C) by the end. Kraeusening is sometimes employed, but often the beer is simply racked into the lager tanks and residual fermentable sugars are relied upon to carbonate the beer. Lager times are often shorter than in Czech breweries, though still long by American standards; four to six weeks is usual. Filtration almost always is employed, but pasteurization is reserved for bottled beers destined for export.

- Adjunct Pilseners -

As mentioned before, adjunct Pilseners are brewed using a mixed-mash method. Well-modified malt is required for this. The rice or corn grits are mixed with about 10 percent of the crushed malt and slowly raised to a boil. They are boiled for at least fifteen minutes to gelatinize the starch. Meanwhile the remaining malt is mashed-in at protein rest temperatures of 113 to 130 degrees F (45 to 55 degrees C) and held until the cereal mash is added. This raises the temperature to the range of starch conversion at 150 to 158 F (65 to

15

70 degrees C), and when saccharification is complete, the mash is boosted once more by direct heat before being run into the lauter tun. Boil times are often short, but multiple hop additions are customary, and a definite hop aroma is important to the flavor profile of these beers. Fermentation usually follows the norm for Continental Pilsener, though many breweries try to minimize storage times and may employ artificial carbonation.

Because of the use of adjuncts, the body and flavor of most Dutch and Scandinavian Pilseners are noticeably lighter than those of German or Czech examples, though the balance is usually preserved. In terms of body and flavor, the Dutch and Scandinavian Pilseners are more similar to American examples, while in terms of hop characteristics they lean toward German standards. Hop bitterness and aroma are lower than for the all-malt Pilseners but higher than for American or Canadian beers. Heineken, if it is fresh and has not been light-struck or otherwise mishandled, is an excellent example.

2

Profile of the Pilsener Style

While the Pilsener style of beer is pale-colored, highly carbonated, light to medium in body, and clean flavored with a distinct hop aroma, these characteristics vary widely throughout Europe. In preparing to brew his own Pilsener, a brewer would do well to understand this range and how the style becomes lighter and more delicate farther away from the Pilsener homeland of Bohemia.

PROFILES

- Pilsner Urquell -

Pilsner Urquell must be taken as the standard against which all Bohemian beers—and indeed all Pilseners world-wide—are measured. It is therefore particularly useful to look at some of its characteristics. Keep in mind, however, that some of the most important aspects of the beer's flavor, such as its hop aroma, cannot be quantified in any simple way. The numbers do not tell the whole story.

Original Specific Gravity	1.049 (12.1 °P)
Apparent Final Gravity	1.014 (3.7 °P)
Apparent Degree of Attenuation	69%
Real Degree of Attenuation	55%
Reducing Sugars (as maltose)	1.4%
pH	4.6
Bitterness	11.5 HBUs per 5 gallons; 43 IBUs
Color	4.2 °L
Alcohol Content	3.6% w/v; 4.5% v/v

The chief observation to be made about these numbers is that while some of them (such as alcohol content) are squarely in the middle of the range for Pilsener beers, others are on the extreme edge. The content of reducing sugars is moderate for lager beers, but rather high for the Pilsener style. Original gravity is only a little higher than average, but the attenuation is lower than for most Pilseners. The beer is best described as moderately attenuated. The numbers related to this phenomenon reflect a high content of proteins and unfermentable carbohydrates, which accounts for the full body (mouthfeel) of Pilsner Urquell. Subjective evaluations confirm the full, rich character of the flavor, which is reinforced by a caramel note in the aroma.

The impression of smoothness and sweetness is enhanced by the relatively high level of diacetyl in the beer, which is 0.15 ppm. By modern brewing standards this is on the edge of being objectionable, especially for lagers. In this full-flavored beer, diacetyl is not identifiable as a buttery or butterscotch note, but its level is well over the taste threshold (0.1 ppm) and undoubtedly contributes to the flavor.

The sweet, smooth flavor and palate fullness of Pilsner Urquell is balanced by its hop character, which chemical analysis can only partly reveal. The beer is very bitter, at 43

International Bitterness Units (IBU, which is the same as parts per million of isohumulone). Assuming a 25 percent hop utilization, which is about average with whole hops, this translates into 11.5 Homebrew Bittering Units (HBU) [also called Alpha Acid Units (AAU)] per five gallons. Pilsner Urquell is certainly the most highly-hopped lager I have ever tasted. The other component of its hop character—the aroma—cannot be quantified by analysis of a single component. Nonetheless, it is extremely high, on a par with the hoppiest pale ales.

Another factor in the flavor balance of some beers is their acidity. This can be measured in several ways. The most common is pH, which reflects the actual concentration of hydrogen ions in the beer. Unfortunately, pH does not

Left: Pilsner Urquell (Plzeňsky Prazdroj) and Budweiser Budvar, two of the best known Pilseners from Czechoslovakia. Right: German Pilseners.

correlate very well with flavor. At 4.6, the pH of Pilsner Urquell is high but within the normal range for a lager beer. The titratable acidity (a better measure from a flavor standpoint) is, regrettably, not available for this beer. In any case, even the total titratable acidity is a rather crude parameter since various organic acids have widely differing taste thresholds and flavors. In most finished beers, lactic acid is present in the highest concentration, but this acid has a high flavor threshold and a mild flavor; hence, it has little impact in the taste of Pilsener and most other beers. Kraeusened beers also contain relatively high concentrations of pyruvic acid (as well as acetaldehyde and other "young beer" compounds). However, the most significant acid from a flavor standpoint is acetic acid, which is volatile and has a much sharper flavor, as well as a lower threshold than lactic acid. According to a study performed by Anheuser Busch, most German Pilseners contain acetic acid at levels at or above the taste threshold of 160 ppm. By contrast, no American Pilsener even approaches the threshold level of this compound, which may partly explain why our Pilseners lack the pungency of many Continental examples, including the original.

In terms of appearance, Pilsner Urquell is darker than most of its descendants, measuring 4.2 degrees Lovibond. Subjectively, this is best described as dark yellow or light golden, but demonstrably darker than the pale yellow of most German and Dutch Pilseners. Haze data are not available, but the beer appears sparkling clear when fresh, and because precipitated protein has dropped out during its three-month period of cold lagering, it is practically immune to chill haze, despite its high protein content.

Terminal gravity correlates with the body and smoothness of the beer, as does protein content, which also affects head retention. The protein content of Pilsner Urquell is 0.45 percent, which is quite moderate for an all-malt Continental beer but half again as high as a typical American lager. Objective data on foam stability are not available for this beer, but subjectively, it is excellent.

In summary, Pilsner Urquell has high carbonation, and when poured forms a thick, long-lasting head. Its aroma is dominated by Saaz hops, but the malt also comes through, so its flavor is strong and well-balanced. The malty sweetness includes more than a hint of caramel, but it is well complemented by a strong bitterness without the least roughness or bite. Body is very full. Overall, the beer is exceedingly smooth but has great depth of flavor. It is truly a world classic.

~ German, Dutch and Scandinavian Pilseners ~

While dozens of other pale lagers are brewed in Czechoslovakia (including such notables as Budvar and Micelovice, the antecedents of Budweiser and Michelob respectively), very few are exported to North America, and analytical data on these beers are almost impossible to find in English-language brewing publications. For this reason, and also because it is the prototype of the style, Pilsner Urquell stands both by right and necessity as the representative of Bohemian beer. But there is much more information available for the beers brewed in West Germany, the Low Countries, and Scandinavia. I will discuss these Pilseners in general terms by comparing them to their Czech original. This comparison shows that the objective data correlate quite well with subjective taste perceptions, though again, the numbers do not tell the whole story.

German

Original Specific Gravity	1.047-1.049 (11.7-12.0 °P)
Apparent Final Gravity	1.008-1.012 (2.0-3.0 °P)
Apparent Degree of Attenuation	74-83%
Real Degree of Attenuation	59-67%
Reducing Sugars (as maltose)	N.A.
pH	4.2-4.6
Bitterness	8.0-9.9 HBUs per 5 gallons; 30-37 IBUs
Color	3.0-3.5 °L
Alcohol Content	3.6-4.2% w/v; 4.5-5.2% v/v

Dutch and Scandinavian

Original Specific Gravity	1.042-1.047 (10.5-11.5 °P)
Apparent Final Gravity	1.007-1.010
Apparent Degree of Attenuation	75-82%
Real Degree of Attenuation	60-65%
Reducing Sugars (as maltose)	N.A.
pH	4.2-4.6
Bitterness	5.4-7.5 HBUs per 5 gallons; 20-27 IBUs
Color	2.5-3.0 °L
Alcohol Content	3.4-4.0% w/v; 4.2-5.0% v/v

These Continental Pilseners are better attenuated than Pilsner Urquell, 75 to 82 compared to 69 percent respectively. This correlates quite well with the "dryer" taste of these beers. The greater the attenuation, the lower the content of reducing sugars and unfermentable carbohydrates in the finished beer. Alcohol content is roughly equal to that of Pilsner Urquell, but the alcohol content of a beer can vary over a wide range without affecting its flavor. Of greater significance is the diacetyl content, which, thanks to modern fermentation techniques, can be as low as 0.02 ppm. Like the lower content of carbohydrates, this translates into a lower sweetness, as well as a less complex aroma.

The German Pilseners have a protein content comparable with the Czech beer, varying between 0.45 and 0.62 percent. As might be expected, they seem subjectively to have good body, though in most cases not as much as the Bohemian brew. In general, the German Pilseners can be described as clean, perhaps even "bracing," with full body and malty flavor, but not as rich and sweet as Pilsner Urquell.

By way of compensating for the lower sweetness of a German Pilsener, the bitterness also is lower. German beers with this level of bitterness, however, are not subjectively less bitter than Pilsner Urquell. The balance between sweetness and bitterness is very much the same. Hop aroma is also strong and seems to be even more predominant in the "nose" of some of the German beers. This may be because most German Pilseners do not have a caramel flavor and aroma and are low in diacetyl.

Finally, German Pilseners also are paler in color than Pilsner Urquell. They usually are sparkling clear though I have run across examples that threw a chill haze in the refrigerator. This characteristic bespeaks shorter processing times, but it is only a problem if the beers are served very cold. Foam retention is excellent, as would be expected from an all-malt beer with a high protein content.

The Dutch and Scandinavian Pilseners are similar to the German examples in that they are very well-attenuated. The original gravities are somewhat lower, however. Given the same degree of attenuation, this obviously translates into a lower content of reducing sugars and unfermentable carbohydrates in the finished beer, a dryer flavor and a less full palate. Furthermore, the protein content of these beers may be as low as 0.3 percent, due to the use of adjuncts in the grist. Diacetyl is very low, typically 0.05 ppm or less. The net result is a beer which, in comparison to other Continental Pilseners, is very light in both body and flavor.

To keep things in balance, the hop character of these beers is likewise diminished. Hop aroma is also considerably lower, in keeping with the more delicate character of the beer.

In appearance, these beers are very clear indeed and are usually paler than German Pilseners. The low protein content means that foam retention is not as good as for the all-malt Pilseners, though it is usually adequate in a clean glass.

In conclusion, I want to repeat that the numbers never tell the whole story. Obviously, if you want to brew a particular style of Pilsener beer, you have to stay within the major specifications, e.g., original gravity, attenuation, color, and so on. But at best, those numbers can give only some indication of how the finished beer will taste. Flavor depends greatly on aroma, and aroma is scarcely accounted for in the numbers I have cited. Beers brewed to the same specifications can therefore vary significantly, depending on the particular raw materials and brewing methods used.

3

Brewing Pilsener Beers — Materials and Equipment

What are the specific ingredients and equipment employed in brewing Pilsener? Two points need to be kept in mind: first, this is not a brewing handbook, so many basic steps that would be addressed at length in such a handbook are mentioned here only in passing. Second, my recommendations for materials and methods are not the only ones that will work. I will give you the rationale for my preferences, but you must be the final judge.

INGREDIENTS

Assuming that no mistakes are made during manufacturing, the choice of ingredients largely determines the flavor of the finished beer. It is therefore critical to understand the flavor characteristics that each component imparts. However, factors such as cost, availability, and suitability to the equipment at hand must also be considered.

- Malt -

Barley malt is a most important ingredient in any lager beer, and it is especially critical in Pilseners. Pale malt typically is responsible for 80 to 100 percent of the fermentable matter in a Pilsener wort, and the clean, simple flavor profile of this beer means that its character will be largely determined by the brewer's choice of this most essential material.

The first choice the American brewer must make is between imported and domestic pale malt. There are good arguments to be made on both sides. Domestic malt is invariably cheaper, owing to lower shipping costs. It is available from numerous sources, which means that shortages are unlikely. This is especially important to a microbrewer who may be faced with increased demand for his product. It is almost always possible to get as much domestic pale malt as needed in a few days' time. Rapid delivery and the multiplicity of suppliers also means that if problems should arise (e.g., a shipment arrives in bad condition), they can be solved quickly. The quality is almost always good, in my experience. Only once did I get a sample of substandard (grossly undermodified) domestic malt, and this was from a homebrew supply shop that probably had bought malt intended for the food or distilling industry.

The negative side of domestic malts is that they are not quite up to the standard of the best imported malts, in terms of their pure brewing qualities. This is largely because of the barleys from which they are made. Over the last twenty years, breeding programs have improved American six-row barleys enormously, but they still have a higher total nitrogen (and therefore protein) content and considerably more tannin than the two-row barleys that are used on the Continent. The domestic two-row barleys (e.g. Klages) occupy an intermediate position between the American six-row and European two-row types.

If a microbrewer is inclined to favor the imported malts, he must do his utmost to assure himself a steady supply at a reasonable cost. All brewers should consider whether the malt they propose to use will suit their process. For many years, the trend in Europe has been toward using well-modified malts to brew Pilsener-style beers, but the traditional undermodified malt is still made. If you are committed to an infusion mash (a mash carried out in a single vessel), you must be sure that your malt is fully modified. Undermodified malt virtually demands a decoction mash (a mash in which the various temperature rests are accomplished by boiling a portion of the mash in a separate vessel). The best test is simply to chew a few grains to see if you can detect the hard, steely tips of undermodified malt. But specifications also are helpful to know, particularly the fine-grind/coarse-grind extract difference.

Most American microbrewers and homebrewers use domestic malts in their Pilsener beers. There is no doubt that it is possible to brew excellent beer from such malts, despite the theoretical advantage held by the European varieties. For microbrewers, the two-row malt is slightly more expensive than the six-row; for homebrewers, prices are usually the same. You might wish to do trial brews with different malts and see what differences you can detect in the final beers. Microbrewers making this test should either buy the malt precrushed from the malting company or use the roller mill in their own plant. Crushing malt in a small flour mill, as most homebrewers do, pulverizes the husks to some degree and results in a greater extraction of tannins into the wort. Thus, such a mill may possibly exaggerate the differences between six-row and two-row malt. Also, one must not assume that all two-row malts are superior. The way the malt is handled and cured is equally important.

My view of these issues is that six-row barley can make excellent pale malt, despite its inherent disadvantages. However, the high tannin content becomes an increasing liability when the malt is cured at higher temperatures. The tannins oxidize and polymerize during kilning, and dark six-row specialty malts, when used in large proportions (certainly over 33 percent), impart an obvious tannic edge to the finished beer. Since virtually all domestic specialty malts are made from six-row barley, I would be inclined to favor imported malts for brewing dark beers such as Munich Dunkel or Düsseldorfer Alt. Fortunately, dark specialty malts are used only in very small amounts for Pilseners, and the domestic products are quite suitable.

Probably the most useful specialty malt for Pilsener beers is Cara-pils® (a trade mark of Briess Malting Company), which is the same as cara-crystal or dextrin malt and has a high content of dextrins and high-molecular-weight proteins. It enhances the body or "mouthfeel" of a beer and also improves foam stability. It does not affect color, aroma, or flavor. Extract is comparable to six-row pale malt. Enzyme content is nil. Dextrin malt contains a substantial amount of unconverted starch and must be mashed with pale malt. Normally, it is used in amounts ranging from 7 to 15 percent of the grist.

Vienna and Munich malts are basically identical to pale malt but are kilned at higher temperatures. They increase color, with typical domestic Munich malt being about 10 degrees Lovibond. However, their most important contribution is the rich malty aroma and flavor they impart. These properties virtually define the Vienna and Munich beer styles. In Pilseners, high-kilned malts can be used in very small amounts (certainly no more than 5 percent) to enhance the malt character of the beer. Large quantities are not desirable because they darken the beer too much and skew the flavor balance toward the malt.

In my opinion, crystal or caramel malt is a better choice than Munich malt for enhancing the malt qualities of a full-bodied Pilsener beer. Like Cara-pils®, but unlike Munich malt, caramel improves foam stability and mouthfeel. It is available in several grades, ranging in color from 20 to 120 degrees Lovibond, and the lower grades (20 and 40 degrees Lovibond) are most suitable for Pilseners and impart a sweet, mild, caramel smoothness. Higher grades are too dark and strong-flavored for this style. Only small amounts of caramel malt are used in Pilseners, typically 5 percent or less.

The dark roasted malts (chocolate and black patent) scarcely are used in Pilseners; their color is so intense that only tiny amounts can be used in a pale beer. Chocolate and most black malts also impart a strong, sharp, "roasted" flavor that is inappropriate to Pilsener. However, at least one American maltster (Briess Malting Company) has developed a black malt with a mild flavor, suitable for coloring adjustments. This black malt could be added to a Pilsener to darken it slightly without changing its flavor. This might be useful to a microbrewer who wanted to make a well-hopped all-malt beer but found that his customers resisted it because its appearance resembled that of mainstream domestic lagers. The amount needed would be very small—perhaps as little as 1/20 of one percent. Black malt usually is rated at about 520 degrees Lovibond.

One specialty malt that should be mentioned here is chit malt, which is used in certain North German Pilseners. This malt is not readily available in the United States, so the reader should refer to the discussion of raw barley, which is almost the same from a practical standpoint (see below).

Wheat malt is not a traditional component of Pilsener-style beers, but because it has many desirable qualities it is well worth considering. Its high content of complex proteins and glycoproteins greatly enhances foam stability. Wheat malt also contributes to the body or "palate fullness" of the beer. At the same time, because wheat has no husk, its tannin content is very low. Replacing a proportion of pale malt with wheat malt lowers the tannin content of the finished beer. Wheat malt has an undeserved reputation of imparting a strong flavor. In fact, the typical clovelike taste of the Bavarian wheat beers is not a result of the wheat malt but of the special yeast strains used in fermentation. The flavor of wheat malt is actually quite mild and smooth, and thus wheat malt combines some of the most attractive aspects of dextrin malt and adjunct grains. In addition, it has a high extract potential, and the domestic varieties are high in enzymes.

Wheat malt also has some drawbacks. It rapidly produces haze, especially when it is used in large amounts such as in a typical Weizenbier. In smaller proportions—up to 20 percent—it poses few problems as long as an adequate protein rest is given. The most troublesome property of wheat malt is its physical makeup. The kernels are small, hard, and glassy, and must be crushed quite fine. This demands a high-powered mill (or some hard labor on a handmill), and in addition, the mill gap must be reset before each run. To avoid these aggravations, the brewer might find it worthwhile to buy wheat malt in precrushed form.

- Adjuncts -

The only unmalted cereals that are traditionally incorporated into European Pilseners are rice and corn (maize). Both perform a similar function in lightening the body and malt flavor of a Pilsener. They differ slightly in flavor; corn has a sweet "roundness," while rice is dryer and more neutral in character.

Small-batch brewers may find that the easiest way to incorporate rice or corn is in the form of flakes that have been pregelatinized and are ready to add to the mash kettle. Because these flakes are not manufactured in America and must be imported from Great Britain they are quite expensive and may be cost-prohibitive in small-scale commercial brewing. Instead, microbrewers may want to consider using uncooked adjuncts such as grits, even though this method requires using an additional brew kettle and a more complicated mash. The traditional form of corn as an uncooked adjunct is ordinary corn meal, which is very cheap and readily available. Both yellow and white corn meal are suitable. Rice used as an uncooked adjunct must be ordinary white (debranned) rice, not precooked or "converted." Short-grain rice is preferred; long-grain rice can be used, but it must be milled before cooking. Rice is more problematic than corn because it does not gelatinize at temperatures below 185 degrees F (85 degrees C).

Untraditional adjuncts include unmalted barley, which is equivalent to chit malt used in some North German Pilseners. It enhances foam retention, imparts a smooth finish and need not result in chill-haze. Unmalted barley flakes imported from Great Britain are considerably cheaper than rice or maize flakes and may be worth considering for microbrewers. Whole barley also can be used, but it must be milled and cooked before it is added into the main mash.

Brewers can use any of these adjuncts in quantities up to 20 percent to produce a light, refreshing Pilsener. Higher amounts, however, dilute the flavor too much and diminish the "Old World" character of the beer.

Sugars are another non-malt source of extract, but they are not employed in traditional lager brewing. In my opinion, they have no place in a European Pilsener. The only exception is the small amount of glucose (corn sugar) used in the bottle carbonation of homebrew.

- Malt Extracts and Grain Syrups -

Pilsener is one of the most difficult styles of beer to brew from malt extract. All malt extracts have been caramelized to some degree during manufacture, so it is very difficult to achieve the light color and clean flavor required of a Pilsener beer. The problem is so acute that many extract manufacturers incorporate corn syrups into their "light" or "lager" extracts and beer kits. This lightens the color but only at the cost of malt character, body, and head retention. Fortunately, there are a few exceptions to the rule.

Malt extracts' chief advantages are considerable savings in time, and convenience in brewing. These may appeal to homebrewers and also small-scale brewers who operate in a location where it is inconvenient or impractical to remove large amounts of spent grains (the only significant solid waste product of brewing) or where it is more profitable to allocate square footage to customer seating rather than to the extra brewing vessels and allied equipment required for mashing and lautering.

One drawback of malt extract is that it is much more expensive than grain malt. This is inevitable since, in effect, the brewer is paying the manufacturer to do a large part of the processing. Another disadvantage is that malt extract severely limits recipe formulation. I would strongly urge any potential microbrewer who plans to make Pilsener beers a mainstay of his business to perform some careful trial brews. Beer quality must be the paramount consideration, and you must satisfy yourself that your extract-based Pilsener will meet the standard set by the finest imported and domestic brands.

Grain syrups are a natural accompaniment to malt extract since they are essentially "liquid adjuncts." They also are well worth considering for the grain brewer who wishes

Zatec (Saaz) hop fields in Czechoslovakia, illuminated by a pale winter sun.

to make an occasional batch of light-bodied Pilsener but who cannot justify the complication and expense of a cereal cooker. Corn and rice syrups both are available, as is barley syrup, though it might be slightly harder to locate. As a result of processing, the subtle differences imparted by the choice of grain often are difficult to detect. Of far more importance is the manufacturing process, which must create a product with at least 40 to 50 percent maltose and a substantial content of dextrins and maltotriose. Some grain syrups are almost entirely glucose and produce a thin, dry beer with a cidery flavor.

- Hops -

Traditional Pilsener beer features a strong, fine hop aroma that can only be obtained from the traditional low-alpha or "noble" variety of hops such as Hallertauer, Tettnanger, or Saaz. High-alpha varieties can be used for bittering, but they have a high cohumulone content that imparts a coarse, clinging bitterness. Such hops also often contain sharp-smelling hydrocarbons like pinene, which must be driven off by a long, vigorous boil.

One thing the brewer must keep in mind is that the rate of boil-off depends very much on the vigor of the boil and the design of the kettle. Therefore, some brewers may conclude that the choice of hops for the first addition (forty-five to sixty minutes before the end of the boil) makes no difference to the aroma and flavor of the finished beer. Others may find that they must use noble hops exclusively in order to get the best results. If trial brews are not possible, the latter is obviously the safest course.

For the finish or aroma hops (whether added near the end of the boil, or in the hop back or lager tank), noble hops are absolutely necessary, and the Saaz variety is the overwhelming choice of European brewers. You may wish to try other types such as Hallertauer, Styrian Golding, Tettnanger, Spalt, Perle, or Hersbrucker. Saaz is strongly preferred, however. Its aroma is almost a requisite feature of a "true" Continental Pilsener.

The merits of whole hop flowers versus pellets have been argued in the literature for some years now. There seems to be general agreement that the grinding and compressing process destroys a certain amount of the most delicate aromatic components. On the other hand, once pelletized, the hops are much more stable than the whole flowers and also possess enormous practical advantages. In practice, most microbrewers probably will choose between whole and pellet hops based on their brewing process. One fact of importance to Pilsener brewers is that Saaz hops are much more readily available in pellet form.

Because hop character is so crucial to a Pilsener, the brewer must exercise the greatest care in selecting and storing hops. One difficulty posed by pellets is that one cannot rub them in order to release their aroma and thus evaluate their freshness before buying them. Whatever the form, hops must be stored properly to prevent oxidation. Experiments have shown conclusively that oxidation is the only significant factor in hop deterioration. If hops can be stored in an atmosphere devoid of oxygen, temperature is irrelevant. When hops are stored in normal air, however, temperature and variety determine the rate of oxidation. Most noble hops store very poorly and can lose a substantial proportion of their alpha acid and aromatics in a few weeks if kept at room temperature. They should be kept in a freezer at 0 degrees F (-18 degrees C) if they cannot be packaged in nitrogen or carbon dioxide.

Let me remind you to select hops with a reliable analysis of alpha acid content. Few small brewers have the resources or time to analyze their own hops. The best course is to anticipate your hop requirements and have sufficient freezer storage to purchase all the hops you will need during the autumn; when the new crop becomes available. Selection is best at this time.

- Yeast -

Traditional Pilsener beer is fermented and lagered at low temperatures, which is an important consideration in selecting a yeast strain. Bear in mind that the yeast must be suitable to the process employed. For example, in recent decades, there has been a strong trend toward warmer fermentations that reduce energy costs and processing time. Yeast strains suited for this American-style fermentation may go dormant at colder temperatures.

Another factor of importance to small brewers is the stability of the yeast strain. A yeast prone to mutation may be acceptable to a large commercial brewery that can afford to watch it closely and reculture frequently, but such measures may not be possible for a microbrewer, and are certainly out of the question for most homebrewers. Stability is vital if consistent quality is to be maintained.

Flocculation is another property that must be carefully considered. An ideal yeast stays in suspension and ferments the wort down to the limit, then settles out quickly and firmly once fermentation is over. This is especially important for homebrewers who use bottle fermentation to carbonate their beer because they cannot filter out the yeast. However, these two traits are to some extent mutually exclusive. One factor that can complicate flocculation in the homebrew process is cold tolerance. Some strains of yeast shut down completely and flocculate if the wort temperature drops below a critical point. They then have to be roused back into the wort in order to restart fermentation. Such yeasts virtually require a system of temperature control in order to function satisfactorily.

Attenuation is another key factor. All strains of true lager yeast, unless they are mutants, ferment maltotriose and many minor wort sugars such as melibiose. However, the strength of their enzyme systems varies considerably, and some strains take a long time to finish the fermentation of these complex sugars. This trait is not a disadvantage for traditional lager beers that are carbonated and matured during a long, cold secondary fermentation in the lager tank. However, the modern trend is to finish the fermentation quickly, and for this purpose it is preferable to have a yeast that can finish off the minor sugars in a brief time span.

Finally, the flavor characteristics of the yeast must be considered. Lager beers, including Pilseners, have a clean palate in which the basic ingredients of malt and hops should predominate. Therefore, an obviously estery aroma, such as is typical of most ales, is undesirable, and low fermentation temperatures, as well as yeast strain selection, are necessary to avoid this. Nonetheless, it remains a fact that absolute neutrality is neither possible nor desirable. All yeasts produce a host of by-products in addition to ethanol and carbon dioxide, and therefore the choice of yeast exerts a great effect on the flavor of the finished beer.

Some lager breweries use yeasts that have a slight estery character. But generally the esters are in the secondary rather than the primary flavor component range and impart a very subtle fruity note to the aroma. For example, Anheuser-Busch highly prizes its yeast for its delicate apple character.

As mentioned earlier, Pilsner Urquell exhibits a noticeable, but subtle characteristic of diacetyl. However, the level of diacetyl, one byproduct of yeast, must be highly controlled in a lager beer. As with esters, yeasts vary considerably in regard to this compound. Often brewers must adjust their fermentation system in order to maximize diacetyl reduction with a yeast that is weak in this respect. Optimally, a brewer can select a strong diacetyl reducer as the production yeast.

Fusel alcohols and fatty acids also have strong unpleasant flavors that are undesirable in Pilseners. Fortunately, the low fermentation temperatures used in lager brewing make these by-products less of a problem than they are in ale brewing. Most commercial strains are satisfactory if handled sensibly.

Of paramount importance to Continental Pilseners is the influence of the yeast strain on the primary flavor components, the malt and hops. Many Continental lager yeasts accentuate the sulfury compounds (DMS, for example) that contribute so much to the malt aroma of a beer. (Actually, this is probably a matter of *not* removing these compounds during fermentation, rather than actively creating them.) Some yeasts also emphasize the hop flavor and aroma, probably because they produce larger amounts of acetic and other organic acids. It should be noted that fermentation temperature also has a great influence on these flavor components; nonetheless, it is a well-known fact among brewers that some strains of yeast emphasize the hops, while others emphasize the malt, still others emphasize both, and some emphasize neither. Obviously a Continental Pilsener needs a yeast that accentuates the hops. Full-bodied, malty Pilseners benefit from a sulfury note in the yeast as well, but this is not important if you are trying to make a lighter version of the style.

While I hesitate to recommend specific strains, I want to state here that my experience has convinced me that the choice of yeast is absolutely critical if one wishes to achieve true European flavor in a Pilsener-style beer. Typical American yeast strains simply do not produce the hop and malt flavors characteristic in the Continental brews. I have demonstrated this with duplicate test batches in which the only variable was the pitching yeast. The beer fermented with the yeast of European origin had a stronger malt flavor and tasted as if it had been brewed to a higher hop rate than its counterpart.

All the European lager yeasts I have used were obtained from Wyeast Labs. Other laboratories supplying yeast to microbrewers and homebrewers carry similar strains. The two I have experience with are Wyeast 2042 (Danish) and Wyeast 2206 (Bavarian). The 2042 emphasizes hops and is quite suitable for a light-bodied Pilsener. It is a slow flocculator at normal temperatures of 46 to 52 degrees F (7 to 11 degrees C) but needs temperature control because it flocculates and ceases fermentation if the temperature falls below 40 degrees F (4 degrees C). The 2206 emphasizes malt as well as hops and is quite suitable for full-bodied Pilseners and Bavarian lagers. It is temperature tolerant and settles out well once fermentation has been completed. Both yeasts are good diacetyl reducers and produce only low levels of other by-products.

My recommendation of these yeast strains does not imply that others are inferior. Furthermore, the performance of any yeast depends on its being properly handled and maintained. However, I want to state here for the record that I have never found a dried lager yeast—domestic or imported—that gave professional quality results.

- Water -

One of the grand generalizations of brewing is that soft water is necessary for making lagers, especially pale lagers. This statement is more or less true, but there are plenty of exceptions. Dortmund, one of the great brewing centers of Germany, has a water supply with around 1,000 ppm of total dissolved solids, which would put its water in the "extremely hard" classification. Yet both Pilseners and the famous Dortmund Export style are successfully brewed there. The fact is that the whole concept of water hardness is so vague that it is nearly useless for purposes of evaluating brewing water. What matters is the specific ion content of the water, and the fact is that by adjusting the brewing process, Pilseners can be brewed from vastly different water supplies.

Nonetheless, it is worthwhile to comment on a few specifics to point out some potential difficulties and the corrections that a brewer may need to make. Consider first the *calcium* content. Most brewing chemists believe that this ideally should be in the range of 50 to 100 ppm. The main effect of calcium is to assist in lowering the mash pH into the desirable range of 5.5 to 5.2. There are other ways of doing this, however. In Plzeň, the water contains only about 10 ppm calcium, but the decoction mash effectively lowers the pH into the proper range. It is easy to raise the calcium content of water by adding calcium chloride or calcium sulfate and I would recommend this procedure especially if one is using an infusion mash. But the problem has to be approached empirically. The overriding concern is the mash pH, and the calcium content must be adjusted accordingly.

Magnesium is well known for its dry, bitter flavor, which is especially unpleasant in Pilseners. It is a necessary yeast nutrient, but malt contains plenty of magnesium for this purpose, and the ion should never be added to brewing water.

Likewise, trace amounts of certain other metallic ions such as *manganese, copper,* and *zinc* are necessary for yeast nutrition. Most natural water supplies contain plenty of these, but occasionally brewers find it necessary to add small amounts of zinc sulfate to their wort. Inclusion of some copper equipment in the brewing plant will take care of the copper requirement. I must emphasize that we are speaking about very small amounts of these ions. In general, metallic ions (except calcium) are not wanted in brewing water, and substantial amounts of iron or manganese (which are common in ground water) mean that lime or other treatment will be needed to remove them. Nickel, zinc, and other ions also impart a metallic taste and/or contribute to haze problems.

Sulfate is well-known for imparting a sharp, dry edge to hop bitterness, and this characteristic does not complement the flavor of Pilsener beers. In general, the higher the sulfate content of your water supply, the lower your hop rate must be. Levels under 100 ppm usually are acceptable. The effect of sulfate is magnified and worsened by *potassium* and *sodium*.

Unfortunately, the sodium content of many fresh water supplies has increased in recent decades, partly because detergent manufacturers have replaced phosphates with sodium compounds in their formulations.

Chloride emphasizes sweetness, and in quantities under 150 ppm, it has no adverse effects. For this reason, calcium chloride often is preferable to calcium sulfate for adjusting the mash pH.

Without a doubt the most important ion in brewing water is *bicarbonate/carbonate*. The content of this ion is often called the "total alkalinity" of the water supply. The one firm rule a brewer cannot escape is that pale lagers, including Pilseners, should be brewed from water with low-level total alkalinity—ideally under 50 ppm and certainly not higher than 75 ppm. Levels higher than this cannot effectively be countered during the mash. Fortunately, it is fairly simple to remove excess bicarbonate from most water supplies, either by lime treatment, acidification, or boiling.

Treatment of water for Pilsener brewing should be tailored to the water supply in question. The following treatments should be considered. However, very few water supplies will need all of them.

First is chlorine removal, which is recommended for all water supplies that have been chlorinated. In practical terms, homebrewers can remove all free chlorine by boiling the water. Microbrewers find it more economical to install a carbon filter. Chlorination off-flavors are especially noticeable in Pilsener beers.

Next is the reduction of the total alkalinity (carbonate/bicarbonate ion content). Many municipalities do this when they "soften" the water through lime treatment. Lime is the most economical means of reducing total alkalinity, but the treatment requires a large mixing tank. Lime is also very effective in removing iron. However, most small-scale brewers prefer to boil the water and decant it off the chalk precipitate, or to use acid. The acid should be chosen carefully to be sure that it will not add undesirable flavors. Hydrochloric, lactic, and phosphoric acids (USP or food grade only) are generally suitable.

Other undesirable ions affect the characteristics of Pilsener and must be removed from the brewing water. For example, if you are determined to make a highly hopped Pilsener, you should consider the sulfate and sodium levels of your water supply. These ions can be reduced by running part of your brewing water through a deionizing filter or a reverse-osmosis filter. These demineralizers remove virtually all solids and produce the equivalent of distilled water. I do not recommend complete deionization of the brewing water because it removes the trace elements needed by yeast. It is better to blend demineralized brewing water in order to reduce harmful ions to acceptable levels.

Finally, you may need to restore the calcium content because many of these treatments remove calcium along with other ions. As noted above, calcium chloride or calcium sulfate can be used for this.

Carbon filters and demineralizing filters can be purchased from laboratory and food-industry equipment suppliers. Chemicals for water treatment are available from various chemical supply houses. For details on the various treatment procedures, the reader should consult the brewing manuals listed in the Bibliography.

⁃ Other Ingredients ⁃

Besides malt, adjuncts, hops, yeast, and water, the only materials generally used in brewing Continental Pilseners are clarification aids such as silica gel, Irish moss (copper finings), and polyvinylpyrollidone (known as PVP or

Polyclar™). These materials are readily available through brewing supply houses.

EQUIPMENT

The equipment needed for brewing Pilsener is no different from that required for brewing other lager beers. Several items are optional, depending on the brewer's choice of method and other variables.

◄ Mills ►

A microbrewer may choose to omit a malt mill and buy malt in a precrushed form. This lowers the initial cost of the brewery and may lower insurance costs since the dust generated by grain mills can be explosive. Homebrewers, too, may opt for precrushed malt. Available hand mills do not give as good a crush as a roller mill, so if homebrewers can get their malt precrushed in such a mill, they may find the extra cost well worthwhile.

The chief drawback of not owning a mill is the higher price of precrushed grain. There is also the problem of storage; crushed malt is much more vulnerable to moisture pickup than is whole grain. To keep precrushed malt in peak quality, the packaging must be of a high standard. Another disadvantage of using precrushed malt is that it is only available from a few domestic malting companies. If you want to use imported malt you must be able to crush it yourself.

Assuming the brewer chooses to mill his own malt, the next choice involves the design. Practical experience indicates that a simple mill with a single pair of rollers (minimum diameter eight to ten inches) is adequate for well-modified lager malt. However, undermodified malt such as that used at Plzeň requires a four-roll mill for a good crush.

~ **Brewing Kettles** ~

A brewer may wish to employ the decoction system or the so-called "mixed-mash" method in which some or all temperature boosts are accomplished by boiling a fraction of the mash and returning it to the main kettle. In this case, he will need two mash kettles: a main mash kettle with a capacity at least equal to the batch size, and a second kettle with a capacity of about two-thirds of the main kettle. Note that the mixed-mash method, which must be used in recipes calling for raw cereal adjuncts, requires that both kettles be heated.

If a brewer uses the classic triple-decoction mash system, in which temperature boosts are accomplished by removing a portion of the mash three different times and boiling it, it is theoretically possible to provide heating only for the smaller vessel. This can lower the initial cost of the equipment somewhat. But I recommend that both mash kettles in a decoction system be heatable simply because there are bound to be times when additional BTUs are needed to achieve a particular rest temperature.

Step-infusion mashing, in which temperature boosts are accomplished by heating the mash kettle, requires only a single vessel. This is therefore the cheapest method, both in the initial investment and ongoing energy costs. An unheated mash kettle must be very well-insulated to avoid heat losses during the prolonged rests.

Another decision faced by the brewer is whether to combine the mash and lauter tuns. This is the traditional British arrangement, and the simplicity and economy are very attractive. It makes particular sense for small microbreweries where only one brew per day is made. Separate vessels are worthwhile when two or more brews are made in succession.

Mash tun and lauter tun at the Budweiser Budvar brewery.

Most other brewing equipment depends on the brewer's specific choices. For example, if one uses whole hops, one must have a hop back or strainer to separate them from the wort.

Several pieces of equipment are particularly important in the brewing of Pilsener beer. One is a whirlpool or some other means of separating the trub from the boiled wort. Another is a wort cooler, which gives a rapid drop to pitching temperature. The clean taste of this beer style depends upon a good cold break and trub removal. Also, some method of controlling temperature during fermentation and lagering is very important both to the clarity and flavor of the finished beer. For homebrewers, having a refrigerator or two is very useful; for microbrewers, fermenters with cooling jackets are virtually required.

The design of the wort cooler is of some importance. Because Pilseners show oxidation very readily, it is best to avoid aerating the hot wort. Oxidation of certain wort compounds (called reductones) may permit them to function as oxygen carriers during beer storage, so they actually facilitate staling. For this reason, even more than for sanitation, I recommend closed heat-exchange coolers for microbreweries. For homebrewers, the counterflow design is good provided that sanitation is strict. If you choose an immersion cooler, use it right in the boiler (with the lid on) rather than transferring the wort to a separate container for chilling.

The last point to be made about equipment has to do with the transfer of mashes, wort, and beer from one container to another. Pilsener has a very full, fresh hop aroma, so it is even more vulnerable to air pick-up than other lager beers. Disappearance of hop aroma is the first sign of oxidation, which is followed by the presence of a cheesy character reminiscent of old hops. To avoid these effects the mash and hot wort, as well as the fermenting and finished beer, must be handled gently. Any pump (including the positive-displacement rotary as well as the cheaper impeller types) causes a certain amount of turbulence and aeration. There is, therefore, good reason to favor the traditional tower design for the brewhouse because it allows most transfers of wort to be done by gravity. More importantly, the finished beer should be pushed by carbon dioxide pressure through the filters (if used) into the bright beer tanks. This transfer method actually removes dissolved oxygen from the beer rather than introducing it.

Almost all commercial Pilsener beer is filtered. I urge all lager brewers not to use tight filtration as a substitute for other means of clarification. It is often necessary to filter the fresh beer to remove a slight yeast haze and obtain a sparkling product, but only a light, "polish" filtering should be needed.

4

Brewing Pilsener Beer—
Procedures

Choice of materials and equipment determines which procedures can be used in a particular brewery. For this reason, I recommend that you read this chapter on procedures for brewing Pilsener beer when considering your equipment's capabilities. Both the previous chapter and this one examine the process of brewing Pilsener from different perspectives.

MASHING

The mash method is one of the most debatable aspects of Pilsener brewing. The choice clearly relates to the recipe formulation, which must be determined first. If the brewer elects to use raw cereals as adjuncts, he must use the mixed-mash system as defined in the previous chapter. Most microbrewers and homebrewers prefer all-malt formulations, however, and they can choose between step-infusion and decoction mashing as defined previously. The method selected may depend on the choice of pale malt. Undermodified Pilsener malts virtually demand a decoction mash. On the other hand, six-row malts probably should not be mashed by decoction because the repeated boiling extracts more tannin from the grain husks than the gentler, shorter infusion mash.

In other words, with undermodified, two-row malt, use the decoction process. With well-modified, domestic six-row malt, use step-infusion. With well-modified, two-row malt, either method will work. In fact, some German breweries now are making pale lagers with what is virtually a single-temperature infusion mash. However, domestic two-row barley has a higher level of protein and beta glucan than the Continental strains, and I believe that some type of multi-step mash, including a protein rest, is desirable with American or Canadian malt.

In most cases, I prefer step-infusion mashing because it is simpler, quicker, and less problematic. The difficulties of decoction mashing include not only tannin extraction but also the danger of scorching the mash during the decoctions. The chief advantage of the method is that it always yields more extract because the boiling bursts and gelatinizes all or most of the starch granules that were not modified during malting. This renders them available to the amylase enzymes that are active during the starch conversion rest. Decoction mashing also gives a lower mash pH without resorting to the addition of calcium because the boiling precipitates more phosphates from the malt.

It is also true that decoction gives a "cleaner" wort, as demonstrated by far less trub in the boiler. This is because the mash has already been boiled so that a large proportion of the proteins, tannins, gums, and other sludge components have already been coagulated and deposited. After boiling, worts produced by either mash method should be very clean. However, it is a fact that more care is needed during the lautering and sparging of an infusion wort in order to avoid bringing unconverted starch into the boiler.

If the brewer chooses the decoction system, he must decide on the number of decoctions and the temperature of the rests to be given. By varying the strike heat of the liquor and the grist-to-liquor ratio, the mash-in temperature can be set at any point. Likewise, by varying the fraction of the mash that is removed and boiled, the temperature of subsequent rests can be controlled. One of the difficulties of decoction mashing is establishing values for these parameters. Variations in the physical characteristics of the brewing equipment make it impossible to follow hard and fast rules; exact procedures must be determined by experience.

In brewing a Pilsener beer, some general considerations influence brewers' choices. One of these is tradition. The traditional Pilsener mash is the classic triple-decoction method. In this system, the grist is mashed-in with a small amount of cold liquor and brought to 95 degrees F (35 degrees C) with an infusion of boiling liquor. After an "acid rest" at this temperature, one-third of the mash is removed, brought to a boil [with a rest at 158 degrees F (70 degrees C) for saccharification] and returned to the mash kettle to raise the temperature to 122 degrees F (50 degrees C) for protein conversion. Subsequent decoctions raise the mash temperature to 149 degrees F (65 degrees C) and finally to 168 degrees F (75 degrees C). This is a very long mash process since each decoction involves the following steps: (1) boosting to saccharification temperature; (2) saccharification rest of fifteen minutes or longer; (3) boost to boiling and, finally; (4) a fifteen minute boil. With each decoction, starch that would otherwise be lost is rendered available. Also, the repeated boiling progressively lowers the pH. Then, after the boiling fraction of mash is returned to the main mash, a rest of twenty minutes or longer is given to allow the enzymes to do their work. This means that it is hardly possible to run a triple-decoction mash in less than five or six hours.

Jean deClerck observed in his *A Textbook of Brewing* (Chapman-Hall Ltd, 1957) that this mash method has been criticized as being too intensive. It is ideal for the specific materials used in Plzeň; i.e., low-calcium mash water (which requires that other measures be taken to lower the pH) and undermodified malt. It is unnecessary with more normal water supplies and well-modified malt. The norm for brewing Pilsener in Germany is a two-step decoction process with the mash-in at protein rest temperatures.

Other variations are even quicker. For example, some brewers use a single-decoction mash in which the boost to saccharification is accomplished by decoction but the final boost to mash-out at 168 degrees F (75 degrees C) is done by directly heating the mash-tun. This program is arguably more sensible than the double-decoction method because starch released during the second boil may not be converted during the mash-out rest (the amylase enzymes are rapidly destroyed at such temperatures) and might cause hazes in the wort and finished beer. However, both methods have been shown to work well with fully modified malt.

Decoction mashing requires planning and experience, and I recommend that you read *Brewing Lager Beer* by Greg Noonan (Brewers Publications, 1986) for a complete discussion of the process. However, I would like to offer a couple of suggestions to beginners. First, all the experts recommend removing the thickest part of the mash for boiling. But do not make the decoction so thick that it is hard to stir effectively because the slightest scorching may ruin the finish of a Pilsener. Scorching is not such a problem in a kettle heated by pressurized steam, and traditionalist microbrewers who want to make Pilseners with the decoction method should seriously think about investing in a steam generator.

The second suggestion is, don't make your decoction too small. If you are not sure how much it takes to achieve a particular temperature rest, guess high rather than low. This is especially important if you are using a main mash kettle that cannot be heated. It is always possible to add the decoction to the main mash a little at a time, and to cool it, if necessary, in order to get the rest temperature you want. But if you take too little, there is not much you can do to rectify the situation.

I must restate my preference for infusion mashing with domestic malts. Infusion mashing is simple and has been well-described in the standard reference works. Furthermore, domestic malts are quite well-modified, and the difference in extract yield between decoction and infusion is not likely to exceed 2 percent. But is step-infusion mashing necessary in order to provide a protein rest? Recent research indicates that relatively little protein degradation takes place in the mash, regardless of temperature. One consideration that complicates the issue is that other substances besides protein are degraded at the low-temperature rest, particularly beta glucans and other gummy carbohydrates. American barleys contain large amounts of these substances, which can cause hazes and a slow runoff in the lauter tun. For this reason, a low-temperature rest may be useful even if proteins have been adequately broken down during malting. Following is a temperature program optimal for each enzyme group:

- mash-in and fifteen-minute rest at 113 degrees F (45 degrees C), which is optimum for peptidase,
- fifteen-minute rest at 140 degrees F (60 degrees C), which is optimum for glucanase and protease,
- rest at 150 F (65 degrees C) until starch conversion (confirmed by iodine test),
- rest for five minutes at 168 degrees F (75 degrees C), which is mash-out.

In my own brewing I follow a simpler schedule, involving only a single low-temperature rest at 131 degrees F (55 degrees C) for thirty minutes. This temperature is not optimal for any of the enzymes, but it is a good compromise. When I use wheat malt, I lower the rest temperature to 122 degrees F (50 degrees C) to favor protein degradation (most important with this grain) and lengthen the time to forty-five minutes.

Pilseners are usually dry, well-attenuated beers so I generally favor a starch conversion temperature on the low end of the scale. For the same reason, a low mash pH, which favors beta amylase, is helpful. However, these recommendations may have to be modified according to the brewer's experience, the materials he has to work with, and the exact results desired.

Some breweries omit the mash-out rest, but I believe this is a mistake. The wort runs off much more readily at 160 to 168 degrees F (71 to 76 degrees C), and sparging is therefore quicker and extraction is often higher if a mash-out is used. At the same time, in doing an infusion mash, it is very important that the sparge water temperature not be allowed to rise over 168 degrees F (76 degrees C). If it does, unconverted starch washes through into the sweet wort, which increases the chance of problems with haze and certain types of amylolytic microorganisms. Anheuser-Busch uses a sparge water temperature of 163 degrees F (72 degrees C), which is just about ideal for infusion or mixed mashes.

The mixed mash method is used only with uncooked cereal adjuncts. The procedure is well-described in standard textbooks and need only be outlined briefly here. The malt is milled and about 10 percent of it is mixed with the rice or corn meal. This mixture then is infused in cold water, which is raised to the starch conversion temperature of around 155 degrees F (68 degrees C) and held for fifteen to thirty minutes.

The purpose of this rest is to allow the malt amylases to saccharify the loose starch before the porridge is boiled. This reduces problems with sticking but the mixture must still be stirred frequently throughout the process. Then the heat is raised, and the cereal mash is boiled for at least fifteen minutes. Longer times may be needed with rice, as this starch does not gelatinize as readily as corn starch. After the cereal mash has been through starch conversion, the main load of malt is mashed in and held at protein rest temperatures for about half an hour. The exact temperature is not very important and should be set so that the addition of the cereal mash to the main mash raises the whole to the desired temperature for saccharification. As in the decoction method, a mixed mash requires experimentation before you achieve consistency in your procedures because equipment and the recipe variations make it almost impossible to count on fixed rules or formulas.

I advise beginners to make the main mash as thick as it can be initially, but to make the cereal mash thin because the grits absorb a lot of water as they are brought to a boil. I suggest three quarts of water for every pound of grain. You may wish to experiment with this. As with decoction, add the cereal mash slowly and keep track of the temperature so that you don't overshoot and destroy the malt enzymes.

In reading these pitfalls of a mixed mash, you may be thinking that flaked adjuncts are a reasonable choice. Any type of flake may be used in either a decoction or an infusion mash, though obviously they are preferable (in terms of saving time and work) in the latter. Flaked corn and flaked rice contain little protein or gum and can be mixed with hot water and added to the mash before the starch conversion begins. However, it is easier just to mix them into the grist before mashing in. Note that flaked barley *must* be handled in this way because it is rich in haze-forming components and needs the benefit of a low-temperature rest.

Sparging technique is no different with Pilsener mashes than with any others. An extra measure of caution is required because, as with other pale beers, Pilseners are highly susceptible to haze. The sparge water temperature must not be too high. Also, the pH of the runoff must not be allowed to get above 6.0 and preferably not above 5.7, particularly when the grist is based on six-row or domestic two-row malts.

The last question to be addressed in this section has to do with the clarity of the runoff. It is my strong belief that, because pale beers such as Pilsener must be as clear as possible, it is vital to recirculate the first runnings until the filter bed is well established and the runoff is reasonably clear. Of course, the first runnings will have some protein haze, but this should be very slight once the filter is settled. If the first runoff is not recirculated, grits and fine-ground pieces of husk are bound to wash into the boiler. This increases the chances of starch and tannin hazes and astringency in the finished beer.

BOILING AND COOLING

In brewing Pilsener beers, boil time is an issue mainly because of its effect on wort color. In Plzeň, the wort is boiled for two hours, but Pilsner Urquell is darker than most examples of the style, and a shorter boil makes it easier to get the lighter color of a typical Pilsener. Some breweries boil under pressure for only a few minutes, but for ordinary boiling at atmospheric pressure, a time of at least forty-five minutes is needed to get an adequate hot break. I usually boil the wort for seventy-five minutes, adding the first lot of hops after thirty minutes of boiling. The reason for this procedure is to get maximum coagulation of the wort proteins with the harsh, astringent malt tannins before adding hops (the other major source of tannin in beer). However, I have not been able to verify the effectiveness of this procedure. The total time is short enough to minimize wort darkening, even with a direct-fired kettle.

When brewing with malt extract, even shorter boils are called for. To avoid darkening and caramelization, I suggest a maximum boil time of forty-five minutes. Extract worts begin to break even before reaching the boil, so boils as short as 15 minutes are quite adequate when you are using pelletized hops.

It is customary in some breweries to add the first lot of hops before the wort reaches the boil. The hops hold down foaming and minimize the danger of a boilover. This may be necessary if the boiler capacity is close to the batch size. However, if the boiler is at least 25 to 30 percent larger than the volume of wort that is run into it, boilovers can be avoided simply by regulating the heat under the copper. In order to save time, most breweries begin applying heat as soon as the sweet wort covers the bottom of the boiling kettle. The wort reaches the boil as soon as the copper is filled. For Pilsener brewing, especially when using a direct-fired kettle, I advise caution with this procedure. The first runnings are of high gravity and are easily caramelized, or even scorched. A few experiments may be needed to determine when the boiler can be fired up without darkening the wort.

At Plzeň, hops are added in three stages over the course of the boil. This procedure gives a full hop flavor because different fractions of the hop aromatics are retained according to boil time. The customary method for imparting the characteristic hop aroma to Pilsener is to add the last fraction of "finishing" hops either shortly before (say five minutes) the end or at the very end of the boil. Some brewers add their finishing hops to the hop back instead.

In the equipment section, I have already discussed the various options for removing the hops from the wort and cooling it. The main point is to avoid oxidation of the hot wort. Some American breweries use open-air cooling in order to maximize the evaporation of certain sulfury compounds (especially DMS) from the finished beer. But since small amounts of these compounds are part of the flavor profile of typical European Pilseners, there is no reason to go to extremes in order to remove them. Also, in a small-scale operation, it is relatively easy to get all the wort chilled shortly after the boil, and once the wort is cool, DMS is no longer formed. In fact, homebrewers using an immersion cooler in the boiler may want to let the hot wort sit for a short time, in order to increase the DMS content of their European-style Pilseners.

The final step that needs to be considered in wort processing is trub removal. This is important because it greatly affects the flavor of the finished beer. To minimize fusel alcohol production, all the hot break must be removed before fermentation begins. Furthermore, it is advantageous to remove a large proportion (at least 40 percent) of the cold break as well. This further reduces fusel alcohols and make it unnecessary to skim the kraeusen of the fermenting beer.

The usual procedure is to run the hot wort through a hop back (if whole hops are used) and into a whirlpool, where the break material collects in a compact mass at the bottom of the tank. Then the wort is chilled and run into a starting tank where the yeast is pitched. During the lag period, the cold break partially settles, and this sediment is left behind when the wort is racked once more into the primary fermenter. This system works well and gives very clean beers. The only problem I can see is that it requires an extra fermenting vessel (the starter tank).

At Plzeň, coolships are used, but the wort is first run through a closed heat exchanger (which avoids wort oxidation), and the main function of the coolship is to allow cold break material to form and settle out before the wort is pitched. I suggest a simpler alternative for small-scale brewers: use a whirlpool, but chill the wort before whirlpooling it. Like the Plzeň coolships, the whirlpool then removes both hot and cold break material and allows the wort to be pitched in the primary fermenter. Also, I suggest chilling the wort as much as possible, down to 40 degrees F (4 degrees C) at least. This reduces the need for subsequent measures to remove chill haze, which is a major problem with all-malt Pilsener beers. The only drawback to this method is that there is a greater accumulation of break material in the heat exchanger so that more frequent cleaning is necessary. Also, the cooler may need to be slightly larger because the deposition of sludge reduces its efficiency.

FERMENTATION

The traditional fermentation of Pilsener beer is a long, slow process requiring three months or more. Pilsner Urquell is still made in this way, and the finished product is a testimony to the efficacy of this system. On the other hand, economic pressures have forced most breweries to adopt shorter schedules in order to maximize their output. Fortunately, scientific research has explained many of the mysteries of fermentation, and greater understanding of the process has enabled brewers to reduce fermentation time without compromising the quality of the beer. However, there are limits. Pilseners with the traditional European flavor cannot be produced by a two- or three-week fermentation cycle.

One trend in modern lager brewing is the use of a separate starter tank, as described previously. The wort usually is held in this tank during the lag phase at a relatively high temperature, perhaps 60 or 65 degrees F (15 to 18 degrees C). The wort is cooled to fermentation temperature after yeast activity begins. This can cut a full day off production time. However, careful monitoring is required or esters and diacetyl may be increased. The traditional fermentation method is to pitch the yeast into the wort at 40 to 48 degrees F (4 to 8 degrees C). This guarantees minimum production of diacetyl, but it also gives a long lag period. In order to get a reasonable fermentation (six to ten days), it is important to pitch a large amount of strong, active yeast. Pitching rate should not be less than 0.67 to 1.3 fluid ounces of slurry per gallon (20 to 40 fluid ounces per U.S. barrel).

The trend in America is toward relatively warm fermentations, typically around 55 degrees F (12 degrees C). This shortens fermentation time, and with a suitable yeast, esters and other byproducts are not noticeable in the finished beer. Nonetheless, the flavor is affected. Acetic acid and

Primary fermentation in oak tubs at the Pilsner Urquell Brewery.

Open fermenters at the Protivin Brewery, Czechoslovakia.

DMS, for example, are actually lowered by a warm fermentation, and these compounds are part of the characteristic flavor profile of European Pilseners. For this reason I recommend that the wort temperature be no higher than 50 degrees F (10 degrees C) during the initial stages of fermentation.

The traditional method of brewing Pilsener calls for a temperature held steady throughout primary fermentation, after which the beer is racked to the lager tanks while secondary fermentation is still in progress. This is in sharp contrast to a newer method wherein the temperature is allowed to rise to about 53 degrees F (11 degrees C) as fermentation progresses. The beer is often held in "ruh storage" for twenty-four to forty-eight hours after fermentation before being transferred to the lager tanks. This allows the yeast to reduce diacetyl to below threshold levels before the beer is racked and lagered. Lagering is not required to mature the beer's flavor and is used mostly for clarification. With the traditional method, several months of cold secondary fermentation are needed before diacetyl is reduced and the terminal gravity of the beer is reached.

One part of traditional Pilsener brewing technique that continues to be popular is *kraeusening*. This is used mainly for carbonation, but it has other purposes as well. For one thing, the introduction of fresh, active yeast at the end of fermentation gives a boost to the diacetyl reducing process. Just as important, it tends to give a more complete fermentation, which means a lower terminal gravity and a dryer finish to the beer. At the same time, the content of certain "young beer" components (such as acetaldehyde) is increased in the finished beer, which may or may not be desirable.

While kraeusening is an excellent technique, it is not always practical, especially for small-scale brewers who do not often brew Pilsener. It is quite possible to get a true Pilsener flavor without kraeusening, especially because the modern fermentation system tends to give some of the same benefits (diacetyl reduction, complete fermentation). Both natural and artificial carbonation can be used, with the latter typically taking place very late in the process, after lagering has been completed. Natural carbonation without kraeusening is very simple, especially when using pressure-resistant tanks for secondary fermentation. The only point to remember is that, if a brief storage time is desired, the temperature should not be dropped as soon as the tank is sealed. The young beer should be allowed to ferment out at 53 degrees F (11 degrees C) before the thermostat is lowered.

It has been mentioned in passing that lagering traditionally served three purposes: clarification, carbonation, and flavor maturation. The last of these can be largely eliminated by modern fermentation technique, as outlined above, and the second can be done artificially. It might therefore be supposed that by the use of filters for clarification, lagering could be eliminated entirely. This may be true in theory, but it does not work out well in practice. Young unfinished beer contains so many yeast cells that an enormous amount of filter material would be necessary to remove them. Also, filters work by *adsorption* (gathering particles on a surface in a condensed layer) and are quite indiscriminate. Yeast cells are so small that they cannot be filtered out without also removing a certain amount of protein material that is important for the head retention, flavor, and body of the finished beer. Therefore, if the brewer aims to make a full-flavored, traditional Pilsener, his only choice is to allow most of the yeast to drop out naturally during lagering and thus minimize the need for filtration.

The time needed for lagering depends on many factors. One is the flocculation characteristics of the yeast; obviously, the faster the dropout after fermentation, the shorter the lagering time. Many breweries use fining agents to enhance the dropout rate. Isinglass, which is very popular in British ale brewing, is not used much in lager brewing. One popular, traditional method is the addition of beech or other hardwood chips to the lager tank. These provide an ideal surface for the yeast cells to adhere to and thus speed up the clarification process considerably. The only drawback is that they are difficult to clean and sanitize. Aluminum "chips" also work and are much easier to maintain, but they are not as effective as the wood chips.

Another factor that influences lager time is the quality of the malt. In order to get a sparkling clear Pilsener, more than the yeast must be eliminated. Colloidal haze, whose chief constituents are protein and tannin, also clouds beer. Haze slowly continues to form and settle out at any temperature, but it forms much more rapidly at low temperatures—hence the well-known phenomenon of chill haze. In any case, haze continues to form in the lager tank, but the amount of haze depends greatly on the amount of haze precursors in the beer. Higher quality malts contain less protein and tannin than those of lesser quality, and therefore require less lagering time. Dr. George Fix, author of *Principles of Brewing Science* (Brewers Publications, 1990), is of the opinion that four to five weeks of lagering is optimal for beers brewed with Continental two-row malt; five to six weeks for beers brewed with American two-row malt; and seven to eight weeks for beers brewed with six-row malt.

Shorter lagering times are certainly possible, and indeed, many American brewing companies do not use a traditional cold lager process. The beer is aged for two to three weeks at fermentation temperature to allow the yeast to settle at least partially, and the beer is chilled briefly (perhaps for twenty-four hours) just before it is filtered and packaged. This method relies on the filters, along with treatments that remove precursors, to eliminate colloidal haze.

⚊ A Note on Lagering for Homebrewers ⚊

The discussion of lagering above is aimed mostly at microbrewers and at homebrewers who serve most of their beer on draft from stainless steel "soda" kegs. These kegs are ideal lager tanks, built to withstand pressure, and a draft system makes it easy to apply polish filtration (if necessary) at the end of the lager period, using carbon dioxide (CO_2) pressure to push the beer through the filter into another keg. This places them in essentially the same position, with the same resources, as their commercial brethren.

On the other hand, homebrewers who use the simple, old-fashioned technique of priming (or kraeusening) and bottle fermentation for carbonation, face a different situation. They cannot rely on filtration at all and therefore must use other means to achieve clarity of their finished beers. In my view, the ideal way of dealing with this problem is to ferment the beer out and then rack to a carboy or other closed fermenter to allow partial settling of the yeast. Dry hopping can also be done at this stage, and clarifying agents such as Polyclar™ can be added. This settling period should be not less than five days, and two weeks is preferable. At the end of this time, the beer should be primed, bottled, and stored at fermentation temperature for at least a week to allow the bottle fermentation to take place. At this point the beer should, if possible, be put into cold storage for one to two months. At the end of this time the beer should be clear when warmed to serving temperature, though it may still be hazy at the 32 to 34 degrees F (0 to 1 degrees C) lager temperature.

The idea here is to regard each bottle as a miniature lager tank. It is possible to make Pilseners with a true European flavor with this system. In fact, if the wort was well-chilled before pitching, and you are willing to apply a dose of Polyclar™ in the carboy, you can get a clear, chillproofed beer even if it is stored at fermentation or cellar temperature. The problem is that there is always a bit of oxygen pickup with home bottling (unless the bottling is done from a draft keg using a counterpressure filter), and the first thing that goes when beer is oxidized is the hop aroma. Therefore, it is better to store homebrewed Pilsener cold, if for no other reason than to forestall oxidation.

FILTRATION AND CLARIFICATION

A light, polish filtration is generally required to get a sparkling, clear Pilsener. A four-micron filter generally will do an adequate job unless the beer has not been properly lagered and handled. Only a minimum of filtration should be necessary. A hazy beer clogs the filters in short order, leading to air pickup and the resulting destruction of delicate hop aroma.

Air pickup must be avoided at all costs. For this reason I recommend that microbrewers use the same system as homebrewers; that is, push the carbonated beer through the filter with CO_2 pressure while maintaining a slight bleed in the bright beer (receiving) tank, which has been filled with CO_2 beforehand. With this system, dissolved oxygen is actually removed from the beer during transfer. By contrast, all types of pumps introduce some air into the beer.

The need for clarification, like filtration, can be kept to a minimum by sound brewing practices. I have found that chilling the wort as much as possible after boiling, in order to maximize the formation and precipitation of cold trub, greatly reduces the need for clarifiers later on. However, Polyclar™ is very useful with American malts as it selectively adsorbs polyphenols (tannins) from the fermented beer and reduces chill haze considerably. Polyclar™ powder can be added to the lager tank after chilling, or treatment can be combined with filtration by selecting a filter element that is impregnated with the compound. The only drawback is that it adsorbs isohumulone to a slight degree and so reduces hop bitterness. This must be compensated for in the recipe formulation.

The other compounds used to clarify and chillproof beer work by adsorbing or breaking down protein. Since this affects the mouthfeel and head retention of the finished beer, I consider these compounds less desirable than Polyclar™. However, with beers that have a severe haze problem, a combined attack may be needed, and silica gel (which adsorbs protein) may be added to the lager tank along with

Polyclar™. Protein-degrading enzymes, such as papain, also are employed sometimes. However, they are hard to control, so unless the beer will be pasteurized (which deactivates the enzymes after a definite period), they must be regarded as a second choice.

BIOLOGICAL STABILITY

Pilseners are especially susceptible to showing off-flavors in the finished beer. Therefore, sanitation is the first line of defense against biological hazes from bacteria or yeast. Without proper sanitation, all subsequent measures are likely to fail.

Beyond sanitation measures, active yeast works against other organisms competing with it, creating chemical conditions that favor its own survival. This means that one of the best ways of assuring the biological stability of a finished beer is not to remove the active yeast. It is common knowledge that filtered homebrews are much more prone to infection than those primed and bottled with active yeast. The problem is that bacteria are much smaller than yeast cells, and the light polish filtration recommended for removing yeast haze and yeasty, "young-beer" flavor notes from Pilsener does not remove completely the lactobacilli and pediococci that can wreak havoc on Pilsener flavor and clarity. There are basically three techniques that can be used to avoid the problem.

The first is the conservative method used (of necessity) by many homebrewers; either don't filter or filter very lightly so that some live yeast remains in the beer, then keep the beer cool and drink it quickly. Most American breweries do not pasteurize their draft beer because they know it will be stored under refrigeration and consumed within a week after it is racked. Brewpubs can follow the same approach.

The second method is to pasteurize the beer. Most European Pilseners exported to the United States are pasteurized, as are most domestic bottled beers. Pasteurization can assure long-term biological stability if carried out properly. At Plzeň, bottled beer exported to Western Europe is pasteurized at 145 degrees F (63 degrees C) for thirty minutes. Beer shipped to America is pasteurized for sixty minutes in order to give it a greater degree of stability commensurate with the long sea voyage and extremes of temperature it is likely to encounter. The problem with pasteurization is that the high temperatures used greatly accelerate oxidation, which leads to stale, winey or cardboardy flavors, as well as destruction of the fine, fresh-hop aroma so vital to a Pilsener. If bottled beer is pasteurized, there are three points to remember:

1) the wort and beer must be maintained in a reduced (unoxidized) state as much as possible at every stage of production or pasteurization can bring about oxidation even though there was no dissolved air in the beer when it was bottled;

2) beer must not be aerated during bottling, and air must be eliminated from the headspace, which means using a good counterpressure bottle filler and knocking the bottles before capping; and

3) pasteurization should be carried out at the lowest temperature for the shortest time needed to achieve biological stability (flash pasteurization is particularly attractive but, since it is applied prior to bottling, sanitation in the bottling plant must be very carefully attended to).

The third method of attaining biological stability is sterile filtration but, because this has the net effect of stripping out much of the body and flavor, this process is entirely inappropriate for any European style of lager beer, including Pilsener.

SERVING

When they bottle, homebrewers face the problem of flat beer that must be primed in order to bring about a bottle fermentation that will carbonate the beer. The problem can be overcome by a two-step procedure. First, fill the bottles carefully to a rather high level. Leave only about five milliliters of air in the neck of each bottle; this means filling a standard longneck to the line that marks the bottom of the bulge beneath the lip. Second, carefully place the bottle caps on all the bottles after filling, and let them sit for half an hour before crimping the caps down. This allows the priming fermentation, which begins immediately, to displace the air in the headspace with carbon dioxide. This gas is heavier than air and therefore tends to expel it. This trick adds time to the bottling procedure and requires an extra degree of

The finished product is available here. A wealth of roadside cafes offer travellers a chance to buy Czech beer before crossing the East German border.

caution to avoid knocking off the caps while they are being crimped. But I have proved its worth in my own brewing. As of this writing, I still have in my basement a few bottles of Pilsener that were bottled six months ago. The beer was made using standard, primitive homebrewing techniques, including glucose priming and bottle carbonation. Nonetheless, this beer maintains a fresh hop aroma after half a year of storage.

On draft, European Pilsener tends to draw slower than American lager because of its greater viscosity. This must be accepted. Increasing gas pressure on the keg will not speed up the flow appreciably.

The temperature at which Pilsener is served is critical because low temperatures numb the taste buds and high temperatures do not allow the beer to remain well-carbonated as a Pilsener should be. In my opinion, a serving temperature of 45 degrees F (7 degrees C) is ideal for this style of beer. Microbrewers and brewpubs may have to educate their customers (including bar owners) about the taste advantages of this relatively high serving temperature. Homebrewers face no resistance but their own to the higher temperatures, but they may need a "dedicated" refrigerator for their beers if they want to maintain the proper serving temperature for Pilsener.

5

Recipes

I am presenting fifteen recipes for four different types of Pilsener beer: Bohemian, German, North German, and Dutch-Scandinavian. These recipes represent the spectrum of Pilseners brewed in Europe—from a rich, malty, well-hopped brew to a light-bodied, refreshing variety. The recipes are of four types: all-extract, designed for homebrewers with a minimum of time and equipment; partial-mash, designed for homebrewers who do not have a full set of mashing equipment but want to incorporate a substantial amount of grain into the formulation; five-gallon all-grain, designed for homebrewers with a complete mashing outfit including a full-size lauter tun and boiler and a wort chiller; and finally, one-barrel all-grain, designed for microbrewers. The one-barrel recipes can be multiplied up to any desired batch size though hop utilization may change drastically in larger batches and may require compensation.

Because it is such a pale beer, Pilsener is very susceptible to subtle changes in the grist formulation. This makes it difficult to create some of the variations with an all-extract recipe. Most special malts and all adjuncts must be mashed, and therefore cannot be used in an extract beer. This means that the extract brewer must rely on grain syrups, which may not have flavor characteristics identical to those of the raw adjuncts. Also, the color may be different and unsuitable for a Pilsener-style beer. I have not by any means tried all the grain extracts on the market, though I can vouch for the malt extracts listed in the recipes. Therefore, I urge all readers who wish to try the all-extract recipes for North German Pilsener or Dutch-Scandinavian Pilsener to carefully assess the "liquid adjuncts" available before using them.

The quantities listed in the all-extract recipes give the stipulated original gravity, but the quantities of grain listed in the partial-mash and all-grain recipes may not, depending on the brewer's equipment and procedures. It is easy to calculate any adjustment required. They are based on what I get in my home brewery, namely, about 35 points S.G. per pound of two-row malt per gallon.

The exact type of boiling hops is not specified in the recipes because several noble types are suitable. However,

The U Pinkasů tavern is less than a block from historic Wenceslas Square in Prague's old town.

Saaz are specified for aroma because they are so much identified with the style. Based on my experience, I recommend dry hopping, and the recipes specify this. For the extract recipes, I recommend hop pellets because they yield their full bitterness with a short boil, which is desirable for minimizing caramelization and darkening of the wort. Also, please note that the hop rates for the recipes assume you are using unhopped malt extract.

Hop rates are based on the rate of utilization usually achieved by homebrewers using a full wort boil: about 25 percent with whole hop cones and 31 percent with pellets. Microbrewers and advanced homebrewers who know what they actually get with their own equipment can calculate the adjustment required to get the results they want. Other homebrewers should try the specified hop rate and adjust it based on their own taste and comparisons with commercial Pilseners.

Hop rates are stated in homebrew bittering units (HBUs), which are the same as alpha acid units (AAUs). International Bittering Units (IBUs), on the other hand, are a measure of the actual bitterness (isohumulone content) of the finished beer. In the one-barrel recipes, I specify the IBUs in order to make it easier for microbrewers to assess and adjust the hop rate (and bitterness, if our tastes are different).

Readers will notice that my recipe for Bohemian Pilsener does not conform to the bitterness specification of Pilsner Urquell. This reflects my experience with my own water supply, which contains 80 to 150 ppm of sulfate. I have made Pilseners using the Urquell hop rate, and the beers had a harsh bite. Brewers must be prepared to alter their recipes, if necessary, in order to accommodate their raw materials. Specifications are the letter of the law, but it is the spirit that must be preserved.

Yeast strain is not specified because several good strains

are available. All of them are liquid cultures of Continental lager yeast, and I have specified these requirements. American lager yeast strains can be considered as a second choice. Dry yeasts are not recommended. A starter culture of at least one pint is *strongly* recommended for homebrewing five gallons and should be made up three or four days before the brewing session.

The priming rate specified in the homebrew recipes gives the correct degree of carbonation for this style of beer. Other methods of carbonation, including kraeusening, are also possible but tend to give more variable results, and rates are best determined from experience. Microbrewers will choose a method of carbonation depending on their equipment and personal preferences.

The one-barrel recipes are less detailed in some respects because microbrewery equipment is quite variable and largely dictates the details of the process. One example is carbonation, as discussed above.

The following recipes can be used with standard techniques as described in many homebrewing and professional brewing texts. The following points should be kept in mind, however, because they are especially critical for success when making Pilsener beers.

1) Pay careful attention to water treatment, including dechlorination (either by carbon filtration or boiling) and ion adjustment.

2) When using specialty malts in extract recipes, crush the grain and steep it at about 150 degrees F (65 degrees C) for half an hour or so. *Do not boil.* Also, do not use dextrin malt or any type of flakes; these grains must be mashed with pale malt.

3) Thoroughly dissolve extract in the kettle *before* applying heat, to avoid darkening the wort. For the same

reason, keep boil time short with extract recipes—forty-five minutes with whole hops, fifteen minutes with pellets.

4) Use a wort chiller if possible, and in any case avoid pouring or stirring the hot wort.

5) Rack the wort off the cold trub, either before or eight to twelve hours after pitching.

6) Pitch the wort at 45 to 50 degrees F (7 to 10 degrees C) with a large quantity of active yeast.

7) If using bottle carbonation, follow the methods discussed in Chapter 5 to avoid air pick-up and oxidation.

8) For the partial mash recipes, homebrewers will need a soup kettle (two gallons minimum) for mashing, and some sort of strainer (again two gallons) for containing the grains during sparging. The mash should be strained into a separate vessel before the strainer is placed above the boiler, and the cloudy first runnings must be recirculated through the bed of spent grains to filter out husks and other solid matter. Sparge with two gallons of water at 160 to 168 degrees F (71 to 76 degrees C). The malt extract is added to the wort after sparging, before the boil commences. Boil time should be one hour.

9) For all recipes that require a mash (full or partial), I recommend the following:

• a water-to-grist ratio of 1.33 quarts per pound;

• a protein rest of thirty minutes at 131 degrees F (55 degrees C);

• a starch conversion rest of ninety minutes at a temperature of 150 degrees F (65 degrees C), *except* for the Bohemian Pilseners, which use 153 to 154 degrees F (69 to 70 degrees C);

• mash-out of five minutes at 168 degrees F (75 degrees C);

• sparge water adjustment to pH 5.7, using food-grade lactic, hydrochloric, or phosphoric acid;

• careful attention to sparge water temperature [on no account higher than 168 degrees F (75 degrees C)].

10) For all-grain homebrew recipes, use four to five gallons of sparge water as needed so that you finish up the boil with five gallons of wort. A boil time of ninety minutes is adequate.

11) Pay careful attention to sanitation at all stages past the boil.

BOHEMIAN PILSENER

Ingredients	Extract (5 gallons)	Mash/Extract (5 gallons)	All-grain (5 gallons)	All-grain (1 barrel)
Malt				
Alexander's pale malt extract syrup	4 lbs.	4 lbs.	—	—
Laaglander light dry malt extract	2.5 lbs.	—	—	—
20°L crystal malt	8 oz.	8 oz.	8 oz.	3.25 lbs. (7%)
2-row lager malt	—	2.5 lbs.	6.5 lbs.	41 lbs. (86%)
Cara-pils® malt	—	8 oz.	8 oz.	3.25 lbs. (7%)
Hops				
Bittering hops	8.33 HBUs pellets	10 HBUs whole or 8.3 HBUs pellets	10 HBUs whole or 8.3 HBUs pellets	62 HBUs whole or 52 HBUs pellets
Saaz (dry hops)	1.5 oz. pellets	1.5 oz. pellets	1.5 oz. pellets	9.5 oz. pellets

Original gravity: 1.049-1.050 (12.5 °P)
Finishing gravity: 1.012-1.013 (3.2 °P)
Priming sugar: 3/4 cup corn sugar (for 5 gallons)
Yeast: Wyeast #2308 or a similar strain. For 5-gallon batch, liquid lager yeast culture ; for 1-barrel batch, 20 fl. oz. yeast slurry.

GERMAN PILSENER

Ingredients	Extract (5 gallons)	Mash/Extract (5 gallons)	All-grain (5 gallons)	All-grain (1 barrel)
Malt				
Alexander's pale malt extract syrup	4 lbs.	4 lbs.	—	—
Laaglander light dry malt extract	2.25 lbs.	—	—	—
2-row lager malt	—	2.5 lbs.	6.5 lbs.	40.5 lbs. (90%)
Cara-pils® malt	—	12 oz.	0.75 lb.	4.5 lbs. (10%)
Hops				
Bittering hops	7.5 HBUs pellets	9 HBUs whole or 7.5 HBUs pellets	9 HBUs whole or 7.5 HBUs pellets	56 HBUs whole or 47 HBUs pellets
Saaz (dry hops)	1.25 oz. pellets	1.25 oz. pellets	1.25 oz. pellets	8 oz. pellets

Original gravity: 1.048-1.049 (12 °P)
Finishing gravity: 1.010-1.011 (3 °P)
Priming sugar: 3/4 cup corn sugar (for 5 gallons)
Yeast: Wyeast #2206 or a similar strain. For 5-gallon batch, liquid lager yeast culture; for 1-barrel batch, 20 fl. oz. yeast slurry.

NORTH GERMAN PILSENER

Ingredients	Extract (5 gallons)	Mash/Extract (5 gallons)	All-grain (5 gallons)	All-grain (1 barrel)
Alexander's pale malt extract syrup	4 lbs.	4 lbs.	—	—
Laaglander light dry malt extract	1.5 lbs.	—	—	—
Barley syrup	1 lb.	—	—	—
Flaked barley	—	1 lb.	1 lb.	7 lbs. (15%) *
2-row lager malt	—	2.25 lbs.	6.25 lbs.	38 lbs. (85%)
Bittering hops	7.5 HBUs pellets	9 HBUs whole or 7.5 HBUs pellets	9 HBUs whole or 7.5 HBUs pellets	56 HBUs whole or 47 HBUs pellets
Saaz (dry hops)	1 oz. pellets	1 oz. pellets	1 oz. pellets	7 oz. pellets

* Crushed raw barley may be used instead. If so, a double mash method must be followed, but the barley must be cooked before the main mash is started. Then the cooked barley must be mashed in together with the crushed pale malt and given a 45-minute protein rest at 131-125°F (55-52°C).

Original gravity: 1.047-1.050 (12.5 °P)
Finishing gravity: 1.009-1.013 (3.2 °P)
Priming sugar: 3/4 cup corn sugar (for 5 gallons)
Yeast: Wyeast #2206 or #2042, or a similar strain. For 5-gallon batch, liquid lager yeast culture ; for 1-barrel batch, 20 fl. oz. yeast slurry.

DUTCH-SCANDINAVIAN PILSENER

Ingredients	Extract (5 gallons)	Mash/Extract (5 gallons)	All-grain (5 gallons)	All-grain (1 barrel)
Alexander's pale malt extract syrup	4 lbs.	4 lbs.	—	—
Laaglander light dry malt extract	1 lb.	—	—	—
6-row lager malt	—	1.5 lbs.	—	31 lbs. (80%)
2-row lager malt	—	—	5 lbs.	—
Brewer's rice/corn syrup*	1.25 lbs.	—	—	—
Flaked maize /rice	—	1.25 lbs.	1.25 lbs.	—
Corn meal/short-grain white rice	—	—	—	8 lbs. (20%)
Bittering hops	5-6 HBUs pellets	6 HBUs whole or 5 HBUs pellets	6 HBUs whole or 5 HBUs pellets	37 HBUs whole or 31 HBUs pellets
Saaz (dry hops)	0.5 oz. pellets	0.5 oz. pellets	0.5 oz. pellets	3.5 oz. pellets

* Note: DO NOT SUBSTITUTE CORN SUGAR.

Original gravity: 1.044 (10.5°P); Finishing gravity: 1.007-1.008 (2°P); 22-23 IBUs
Priming sugar: 3/4 cup corn sugar (for 5 gallons)
Yeast: Wyeast #2042 or a similar strain. For 5-gallon batch, liquid lager yeast culture; for 1-barrel batch, 20 fl. oz. yeast slurry.

Appendix:
Commercial Pilseners

I am listing only a few commercial Continental Pilseners that I have tried recently. Most of the world's Pilseners are of the very light American type, and this includes most of the imports available in the average grocery or liquor store. Even in Europe, many breweries have jumped on the "light" and "dry" beer bandwagons in an effort to increase their sales in North America. As a result, the country of origin is no guarantee of authenticity.

Pilsner Urquell—brewed at the Plzeňsky Prazdroj brewery in Plzeň, Czechoslovakia. This original Pilsener beer is darker, maltier and better hopped than most of its imitators. The technology used for brewing this beer has not changed since about 1870. In this country, Urquell seems to vary quite a bit. Many times it is old and stale with its hop character sadly gone. In good condition, it is one of the world's great beers.

DAB—brewed at the Dortmunder Actien Brauerei in Dortmund, West Germany. This is an excellent example of the German interpretation of the Pilsener style—lighter in color and lacking the caramel note of Pilsner Urquell. It is clean and refreshing, with a full malt flavor well balanced by the hops.

Warsteiner—brewed at the Warstein brewery in Warstein, West Germany. Another fine example of an all-malt German Pilsener. Dry hopping gives it a very fresh, pungent aroma.

Beck's—brewed at the Beck brewery in Bremen, West Germany. Once a fine example of a North German Pilsener, Beck changed its recipe formulation to cater to American taste and take advantage of the loophole in the Reinheitsgebot that allows adjuncts in beers designed for the export market. Though still well-made, the beer today is closer to a Scandinavian-type Pilsener than a German one.

Heineken—brewed at the Heineken brewery in Amsterdam, The Netherlands. A good example of the lighter variety of Continental Pilsener that uses adjuncts in the formulation. Better hopped than some of its competitors in this class and, when fresh, a very rewarding beer.

Carlsberg—brewed at the Carlsberg brewery in Copenhagen, Denmark. Another example of the lighter style of Continental Pilsener. Less hop character than Heineken.

Old German Pilsner—brewed at the Frankenmuth brewery in Frankenmuth, Michigan. An excellent microbrewed Pilsener in the German style. Dryer than most examples of the type.

Glossary

adjunct. Any *unmalted* grain or other fermentable ingredient added to the mash.

aeration. The action of introducing air to the wort at various stages of the brewing process.

airlock. (see fermentation lock)

airspace. (see ullage)

alcohol by volume (v/v). The percentage of volume of alcohol per volume of beer. To calculate the approximate volumetric alcohol content, subtract the terminal gravity from the original gravity and divide the result by 75. For example: $1.050 - 1.012 = .038 / 75 = 5\%$ v/v.

alcohol by weight. The percentage weight of alcohol per volume of beer. For example: 3.2% alcohol by weight = 3.2 grams of alcohol per 100 centiliters of beer.

ale. 1. Historically, a nonhopped malt beverage. 2. A generic term for beers produced by top fermentation, as opposed to lagers, which are produced by bottom fermentation.

all-extract beer. A beer made with only malt extract as opposed to one made from barley, or a combination of malt extract and barley.

all-grain beer. A beer made with only malted barley as opposed to one made from malt extract, or from malt extract and malted barley.

all-malt beer. A beer made with only barley malt with no adjuncts or sugars.

alpha acid. A soft resin in hop cones. When boiled, alpha acids are connected to isoalpha acids, which account for 60 percent of a beer's bitterness.

alpha-acid unit. A measurement of the potential bitterness of hops, expressed by their percentage of alpha acid. Low = 2 to 4%, medium = 5 to 7%, high = 8 to 12%. Abbrev: A.A.U.

attenuation. The reduction in the wort's specific gravity caused by the transformation of sugars into alcohol and carbon-dioxide gas.

Balling. A saccharometer invented by Carl Joseph Napoleon Balling in 1843. It is calibrated for 63.5 degrees F (17.5 degrees C), and graduated in grams per hundred, giving a direct reading of the percentage of extract by weight per 100 grams solution. For example: 10 °B = 10 grams of sugar per 100 grams of wort.

blow-by (blow-off). A single-stage homebrewing fermentation method in which a plastic tube is fitted into the mouth of a carboy, with the other end submerged in a pail of sterile water. Unwanted residues and carbon dioxide are expelled through the tube, while air is prevented from coming into contact with the fermenting beer, thus avoiding contamination.

carbonation. The process of introducing carbon-dioxide gas into a liquid by: 1. injecting the finished beer with carbon dioxide; 2. adding young fermenting beer to finished beer for a renewed fermentation (kraeusening); 3. priming (adding sugar) to fermented wort prior to bottling, creating a secondary fermentation in the bottle.

carboy. A large glass, plastic or earthenware bottle.

chill haze. Haziness caused by protein and/or tannin during the secondary fermentation.

coolship. A flat, open tun placed immediately after the hop strainer and into which the hot wort cools naturally and loses its coarse sludge.

decoction mashing. A brewing method used for bottom-fermenting beers. The process requires three vessels: a mash tun for mash-mixing, a mash kettle (or copper or mash copper) for boiling and a lauter tun (or clarifying tun) for straining. Mashing is carried out in a mash tun and starts at a low temperature while portions of the mash are taken out and boiled in the mash kettle and later returned to the mash tun — thus gradually raising the temperature of the entire mash. The process is usually repeated two or three times and sometimes up to 13 times. The mash is afterwards filtered in a separate vessel known as a lauter tun.

diacetyl. Described as buttery, butterscotch.

direct fired. Flames used to heat the kettle.

DMS (dimethyl sulfide). A compound that may be present in beer that has the character of a sweet, corn-like aroma/flavor.

dry hopping. The addition of hops to the primary fermenter, the secondary fermenter, or to casked beer to add aroma and hop character to the finished beer without adding significant bitterness.

dry malt. Malt extract in powdered form.

extract. The amount of dissolved materials in the wort after mashing and lautering malted barley and/or malt adjuncts such as corn and rice.

fermentation lock. A one-way valve, which allows carbon-dioxide gas to escape from the fermenter while excluding contaminants.

final specific gravity. The specific gravity of a beer when fermentation is complete.

fining. The process of adding clarifying agents to beer during secondary fermentation to precipitate suspended matter.

flocculation. The behavior in which yeast cells join into masses and settle out toward the end of fermentation.

gelatinization. The inhibition of water and the resulting swelling of starch granules when moist heat is applied to starch. It is the first stage in the enzymatic breakdown of starch followed by liquefaction and saccharification.

homebrew bittering units. A formula invented by the

American Homebrewers Association to measure bitterness of beer. Example: 1.5 ounces of hops at 10 percent alpha acid for five gallons: 1.5 x 10 = 15 HBU per five gallons.

hop pellets. Finely powdered hop cones compressed into tablets. Hop pellets are 20 to 30 percent stronger by weight than the same variety in loose form.

hydrometer. A glass instrument used to measure the specific gravity of liquids as compared to water, consisting of a graduated stem resting on a weighed float.

International bitterness units. An approximate (within 20%) method of measuring bitterness in beer based on parts per million content of alpha acids. IBUs are calculated with the following formula:

$$B.U. = \frac{H \times (a\text{-}a + b\text{-}a/9)}{0.3}$$

where: H = weight of hops in grams per liter (H g/l)
a-a = alpha acid percent
b-a = beta acid percent

Bittering units are an internationally agreed upon standard and equal .000133 of an ounce (avoirdupois) of isoalpha acid per gallon of solution or about 1 milligram per liter.

kraeusen. (n.) The rocky head of foam which appears on the surface of the wort during fermentation. (v.) Adding fermenting wort to fermented beer to induce carbonation through a secondary fermentation.

lager. (n.) A generic term for any bottom-fermented beer. Lager brewing is now the predominant brewing method worldwide except in Britain where top fermented ales dominate. (v.) Storing beer at near-zero temperatures to precipitate yeast cells and proteins and improve taste.

lautering. The process of separating the spent grains from the sweet wort with a straining apparatus. Etym: From the German *lauter* meaning clarifying.

lauter tun. A vessel with a false, slotted bottom and spigot in which the mash settles and the grains are removed from the sweet wort through a straining process.

liquefaction. The process by which alpha-amylase enzymes degrade soluble starch into dextrin.

malt. Barley that has been steeped in water, germinated and dried in kilns to convert insoluble starches to soluble substances and sugars.

malt extract. A thick syrup or dry powder prepared from malt.

mashing. Mixing ground malt with water to extract the fermentables, degrade haze-forming proteins and convert grain starches to fermentable sugars and nonfermentable carbohydrates.

modification. 1. The physical and chemical changes in barley as a result of malting. 2. The degree to which these changes have occurred, as determined by the growth of the acrospire.

original gravity. The specific gravity of wort previous to fermentation and compared to the density of water at 39.2 degrees F (4 degrees C), which is given the value 1.000. A measure of the total amount of dissolved solids in wort.

pH. Potential of hydrogen. A measure of acidity or alkalinity of a solution, usually on a scale of one to 14, where seven is neutral.

Pilsener. A general name for pale, golden-hued, highly hopped bottom-fermented beers. The original Pilsner was first brewed at the Bürgerlisches Brauhaus in the Bohemian town of Plzen (meaning green meadow) in Czechoslovakia in 1842. It was then the palest beer available and the style was soon copied worldwide. The archetypal Pilsner is presently known as Plzensky Prazdroj of Pilsner Urquell (Urquell means "original source") and the name was patented in 1898.

Plato. A saccharometer which expresses specific gravity as extract weight in a one-hundred-gram solution at 64 degrees F (18 degrees C). A revised, more accurate version of Balling, by Dr. Plato.

primary fermentation. The first stage of fermentation, during which most fermentable sugars are converted to ethyl alcohol and carbon dioxide.

priming sugar. A small amount of corn or cane sugar added to bulk beer prior to racking or at bottling to induce a new fermentation and create carbonation.

racking. The process of transferring beer from one container to another, especially into the final package (bottles, kegs, etc.).

saccharification. The naturally occurring process in which malt starch is converted into fermentable sugars, primarily maltose.

saccharometer. An instrument that determines the sugar concentration of a solution by measuring the specific gravity.

secondary fermentation. 1. The second, slower stage of fermentation, lasting from a few weeks to many months depending on the type of beer. 2. A fermentation occuring in bottles or casks and initiated by priming or adding yeast.

sparging. Spraying the spent grains in the mash with hot water to retrieve the remaining malt sugar.

specific gravity. A measure of a substance's density as compared to that of water, which is given the value of 1.000 at 39.2 degrees F (4 degrees C). Specific gravity is dimensionless, with no accompanying units, because it is expressed as a ratio.

starter. A batch of fermenting yeast, added to the wort to initiate fermentation.

strike temperature. The initial temperature of the water when the malted barley is added to it to create the mash.

trub. Suspended particles resulting from the precipitation of proteins, hop oils and tannins during boiling and cooling stages of brewing.

ullage. The empty space between a liquid and the top of its container. Also called airspace or headspace.

water hardness. The degree of dissolved minerals in water.

wort. The mixture that results from mashing the malt and boiling the hops, before it is fermented into beer.

Bibliography

Burch, Byron. *Brewing Quality Beers.* Fulton, California: Joby Books, 1987.

Clerck, Jean de. *A Textbook of Brewing.* 2 vols. Translated by K. Barton-Wright. London: Chapman-Hall Ltd., 1957.

Fix, George. *Introduction to Brewing Science.* Boulder, Colorado: Brewers Publications, 1989.

Hough, Briggs, Stevens, and Young. *Malting and Brewing Science,* 2 vols. London: Chapman-Hall Ltd., 1981.

Jackson, Michael. *World Guide to Beer, Second Edition.* Philadelphia: The Running Press, 1988.

Master Brewers Association of America. *The Practical Brewer.* St. Louis, Missouri, 1977.

Miller, Dave. *The Complete Handbook of Home Brewing.* Pownal, Vermont: Garden Way Publishing, 1988.

Noonan, Greg. *Brewing Lager Beer.* Boulder, Colorado: Brewers Publications, 1986.

Papazian, Charlie. *The Complete Joy of Home Brewing.* New York: Avon Books, 1983.

Index

mash, 41-42, 43, 50, 52, 54
Plzeň, 1, 7-8, 12
Pilsener
American, 7, 11, 21, 60-61, 64
adjuncts in, 15-16
all-malt, 14-15
Bohemian, 6-7, 12-14, 17-22, 59,
73; *Recipes*, 77
flavor characteristics, 11-12
German, 3, 8, 23-24; *Recipes*, 78
North German, 11, 31, 33; *Recipes*,
79
Scandinavian-Dutch, 11, 24;
Recipes, 80
Poupe, František, 6
Priming, *See* Carbonation
Protein, 21, 23, 24, 28, 56, 63-64,
66-67
Rice, *See* Adjuncts, flakes
Refrigeration, 10-11, 47
Sedelmayr, Gabriel, 10
Sanitation, 48, 67, 68, 76
Serving, 69-70
Sparge, 50-51, 54, 56
Steam, 8, 10, 52
Sugar(s), 33, 38
glucose (corn sugar), 33, 35, 70
grain syrups, 34-35
maltose, 35
maltotriose, 35
Sweetness, 3, 14, 18, 21, 23, 43
Tannins, 29-30, 50, 56-57, 66
Temperature
control, 38, 47
fermentation, 14, 15, 40, 60-61
hop storage, 37
lager, 65
mash, 12, 15, 51-55, 75

pasteurization, 68
pitching, 14, 15
serving, 64, 70
sparge water, 54
Trub, 14, 47, 58, 66, 75
Water, 41-44, 73
hardness, 8, 41
Plzeň, 8, 52
sparge, 54, 56
treatment, 43-44
See also Ions
Whirlpool, 47, 58-59
Wild yeast, 10
Wort
boiling, 56-57
cooling, 14, 47-48, 58, 65, 66
color, 8, 56
oxidation, 68
Pilsener, 28
scorching, 8, 57
Yeast
American, 40
and bacteria, 67
attenuation, 38
European, 39-41
flavor characteristics, 38-40
flocculation, 38
haze, 48
lager, 7, 38, 40, 74
mutation, 37-38
pitching, 14, 15, 47, 58, 60, 75
pitching rate, 60
selection, 37-41
starters, 74
starting tank, 58, 59
top-fermenting, 7
wheat beer, 32
Yield, *See* Extract

HOMEBREWER?

Get the Whole Story!

Join the thousands of American Homebrewers Association® members who read **Zymurgy®** — the magazine for homebrewers and beer lovers.

Every issue of **Zymurgy** is full of tips, techniques, new recipes, new products, equipment and ingredient reviews, beer news, technical articles — the whole world of homebrewing. PLUS, the AHA brings members the National Homebrewers Conference, the National Homebrew Competition, the Beer Judge Certification Program, the Homebrew Club Network, periodic discounts on books from Brewers Publications and much, much more.

Name _____

Address _____

City _____ State/Province _____

Zip/Postal Code _____ Country _____

Daytime Phone _____

☐ Enclosed is $29 for a one-year membership ($33 after 3/1/96).
Canadian memberships are $34 U.S. ($38 after 3/1/96); international memberships are $44 U.S. ($51 after 3/1/96).

☐ Please charge my credit card. ☐ Visa ☐ MC

Card No. _____ – _____ – _____ Exp. Date _____

Signature _____

Please make check or money order payable to: American Homebrewers Association, PO Box 1510, Boulder, CO 80306-1510, U.S.A. Call (303) 447-0816, Internet orders@aob.org or FAX (303) 447-2825 with credit card orders.

Offer is valid until 2/28/96.   Prices are subject to change.   MEAD

Examine the World of

Microbrewing

and

Pubbrewing

Travel the world of commercial, small-scale brewing, the realm of microbrewers and pubbrewers.

The New Brewer magazine guides you through this new industry. Its pages introduce you to marketing, finance, operations, equipment, recipes, interviews — in short, the whole landscape.

Subscribe to *The New Brewer* and become a seasoned traveler.

No Risk Offer

Subscribe now and receive six issues. Money-back guarantee.

$55 a year (U.S.)
$65 (International)
U.S. funds only

Published by the Institute for Brewing Studies, PO Box 1510, Boulder, CO 80306-1510, USA; (303) 546-6514; Internet orders@aob.org; FAX (303) 447-2825.

The ***New Brewer***
THE MAGAZINE FOR MICRO- AND PUB-BREWERS

BOOKS for Brewers and Beer Lovers

Order Now ... Your Brew Will Thank You!

These books offered by Brewers Publications are some of the most sought-after reference tools for homebrewers and professional brewers alike. Filled with tips, techniques, recipes and history, these books will help you expand your brewing horizons. Let the world's foremost brewers help you as you brew. Whatever your brewing level or interest, Brewers Publications has the information necessary for you to brew the best beer in the world — your beer.

- -

Please send me more free information on the following: (check all that apply)

◊ Merchandise and Book Catalog   ◊ Institute for Brewing Studies
◊ American Homebrewers Association®   ◊ Great American Beer Festival®

Ship to:

Name

Address

City   State/Province

Zip/Postal Code   Country

Daytime Phone   (   )

Please use this form in conjunction with the standard order form when ordering books from Brewers Publications.

Payment Method

◊ Check or Money Order Enclosed (Payable to Brewers Publications)
◊ Visa   ◊ MasterCard

Card Number   –   –   –   Expiration Date

Name on Card   Signature

Brewers Publications, PO Box 1510, Boulder, CO 80306-1510, USA; (303) 546-6514; Internet orders@aob.org; FAX (303) 447-2825.

MEAD

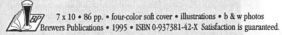

BREWERS PUBLICATIONS ORDER FORM

PROFESSIONAL BREWING BOOKS

QTY.	TITLE	STOCK #	PRICE	EXT. PRICE
_____	Brewery Planner	500	80.00	_____
_____	North American Brewers Resource Directory	505	80.00	_____
_____	Principles of Brewing Science	463	29.95	_____

THE BREWERY OPERATIONS SERIES
from Micro- and Pubbrewers Conferences

QTY.	TITLE	STOCK #	PRICE	EXT. PRICE
_____	Volume 6, 1989 Conference	536	25.95	_____
_____	Volume 7, 1990 Conference	537	25.95	_____
_____	Volume 8, 1991 Conference, Brewing Under Adversity	538	25.95	_____
_____	Volume 9, 1992 Conference, Quality Brewing — Share the Experience	539	25.95	_____

CLASSIC BEER STYLE SERIES

QTY.	TITLE	STOCK #	PRICE	EXT. PRICE
_____	Pale Ale	401	11.95	_____
_____	Continental Pilsener	402	11.95	_____
_____	Lambic	403	11.95	_____
_____	Vienna, Märzen, Oktoberfest	404	11.95	_____
_____	Porter	405	11.95	_____
_____	Belgian Ale	406	11.95	_____
_____	German Wheat Beer	407	11.95	_____
_____	Scotch Ale	408	11.95	_____
_____	Bock	409	11.95	_____

BEER AND BREWING SERIES, for homebrewers and beer enthusiasts, from National Homebrewers Conference

QTY.	TITLE	STOCK #	PRICE	EXT. PRICE
_____	Volume 8, 1988 Conference	448	21.95	_____
_____	Volume 10, 1990 Conference	450	21.95	_____
_____	Volume 11, 1991 Conference, Brew Free or Die!	451	21.95	_____
_____	Volume 12, 1992 Conference, Just Brew It!	452	21.95	_____

GENERAL BEER AND BREWING INFORMATION

QTY.	TITLE	STOCK #	PRICE	EXT. PRICE
_____	The Art of Cidermaking	468	9.95	_____
_____	Brewing Lager Beer	460	14.95	_____
_____	Brewing Mead	461	11.95	_____
_____	Dictionary of Beer and Brewing	462	19.95	_____
_____	Evaluating Beer	465	19.95	_____
_____	Great American Beer Cookbook	466	24.95	_____
_____	Victory Beer Recipes	467	11.95	_____
_____	Winners Circle	464	11.95	_____

SUBTOTAL _____

Call or write for a free Beer Enthusiast catalog today.
• U.S. funds only.
• All Brewers Publications books come with a money-back guarantee.
* **Postage & Handling:** $4 for the first book ordered, plus $1 for each book thereafter. For Canadian and international orders please add $5 for the first book and $2 for each book thereafter. Orders cannot be shipped without appropriate P&H.

Colo. Residents Add 3% Sales Tax _____

P&H * _____

TOTAL _____

Brewers Publications, PO Box 1510, Boulder, CO 80306-1510, USA;
(303) 546-6514; Internet orders@aob.org; FAX (303) 447-2825.

MEAD